Collins

Enhanced English Alive Coursebook 2

Sonia Duggal

Series Editor
Renu Viswanath

Acknowledgements

The publishers wish to thank and acknowledge the following for granting us permission to use copyright material:

Under My Bed, written by Anupa Lal and illustrated by Suvidha Mistry (© Pratham Books, 2015); *No Smiles Today*, written by Cheryl Rao and illustrated by Saurabh Pandey (© Pratham Books, 2015); *Goodnight, Tinku!*, written by Preethi Nambiar and illustrated by Sonal Goyal and Sumit Sakhuja (© Pratham Books, 2014), all published by Pratham Books under a CC BY 4.0 license on StoryWeaver; Eleanor Farjeon for *Bedtime*, taken from *Blackbird Has Spoken*, published by Macmillan. Copyright © The Roald Dahl Story Company Limited; *The Water Seed* by Munda Writers' Group, translated by Amrit Mishra, illustrated by Ramani Ranjan Sarangi (© Pratham Books, 2014), published by Pratham Books under a CC BY 4.0 license on StoryWeaver.

The publishers have applied for permission for the following:
The Bird of Mind by Sayan Chaudhuri adapted as *Piklu and the Mynah*, *Tyltyl's Adventure* by Swapna Dutta.

Acknowledgements for these texts will be made in the future editions of the book.

Every effort has been made to trace copyright holders and to obtain their permission for the use of copyright material. However, in some instances, we have been unable to trace the owners of the copyright pieces published here. The authors and publishers will gladly receive any information enabling them to rectify any error or omission in subsequent editions.

Illustrations

Cover and Title Page: Created by Toonfantasy

Inside: Page 13: Smitt777; **14:** Natalia Darmoroz; **16:** Natalia Darmoroz; **17:** paul_june; **19:** Clive Rees Photography; **28:** vectomart; **30:** KanKhem; **31:** KanKhem; **41:** Ylivdesign, pijama61; **42:** depros, Armation; **44:** Dmitry Volkov; **48:** KanKhem; **50:** skalapendra, lushik, losw, LeeDaniels, Aaltazar; **54:** kbeis; **56:** saemilee, adekvat, Mahfud2015, Aaltazar, nyamol; **66:** Elena Istomina; **67:** Tigatelu, bandian1122, VasjaKoman, TECHDESIGNWORK; **77:** Big_Ryan; **80:** kraphix; **84:** bennyb, kbeis, TECHDESIGNWORK, Lonely__; **99:** draco77, Nina_Piankova, lushik, 9comeback, RedlineVector; **105:** KanKhem; **117:** exxorian; **118:** AlexBrylov, AM29, vishnurajan; **120:** vchal, RamonBerk, Claudiad; **121:** ksenya_savva; **122:** amtitus; **124:** Premiumstock, nicholashan, MarianVejcik; **125:** Davidtalukdar, OksanaKiian, bdspn, miroslav_1, jutka5; **126:** mlharing, davidevison, Danielrao; **131:** P2007;

Preface

Enhanced English Alive is a multi-skill course in English that adheres to the guidelines laid down by the **National Education Policy, 2020**. This edition retains the original essence of teaching communicative English using a cross-curricular approach and interactive and experiential teaching and learning methods. It offers high-quality English language materials with a coherent structured approach, effective integration of subject knowledge and life skills.

The series comprises Coursebooks and Workbooks for Foundational Stage (Nursery, LKG, UKG, Classes 1 and 2), Preparatory Stage (Classes 3 to 5), and Middle Stage (Classes 6 to 8). Literature Readers are for the Preparatory and Middle Stages (Classes 3 to 8). Each grade package includes a Teacher's Resource Pack and a Collins DigiSuite.

This series integrates the essence of **NIPUN Bharat** guidelines, which extensively deal with foundational literacy and numeracy. Each book aims to motivate learners to read independently, to improve their vocabulary, to develop their critical thinking and creative skills, as well as to enhance their ability to express themselves both verbally and in writing.

This series takes care of the requirements of **Structured Assessments For Analyzing Learning (SAFAL)**. Research-based activities and projects have been used to instill inquiry-based learning, while comprehension passages have been followed by extrapolative and value-based questions that involve analysis-based learning. Additionally, in the Middle Stage (Classes 6 to 8), an end-of year question paper is provided which is based on the latest CBSE guidelines.

Key features

Coursebooks

- **Warm-up:** A wide variety of picture-based fun activities or probing questions at the beginning of chapters initiate the learner into the subject and ensure his/her active engagement in the lesson. For grades 1 to 5, these activities are introspective and meditative inquiries that are based on the pedagogy of mindfulness as delineated in the NEP, 2020.
- **Reading:** Each book has well-chosen selections from a wide range of literary genres that are also useful in cross-curricular teaching. These include picture stories and comic strips.
- **Cross-curricular boxes:** This series specially covers topics that are interrelated with other subjects taught in the same grade. Dedicated boxes teaching these cross-curricular concepts are placed along the main text.
- **Glossary:** All new words in the text are highlighted and their meanings are given in simple language using the easiest possible words. Literary devices are also taught along with a glossary of literary terms.
- **Summary:** A short summary at the end of each text is provided for an easy way to remember the essence of the text.
- **Comprehension:** This section includes plenty of exercises including factual, inferential, and extrapolative questions.
- **Life Skills and Values:** There is a separate thematic section on life skills and values aimed at developing good character in students and equipping them with skills needed to cope with

different challenges in life. Guidelines set by NEP, 2020 have been followed in selecting these life skills and values.

- **Vocabulary:** Each chapter has boxed explanations of new vocabulary words and topics followed by a variety of exercises. Spelling is also taught in this section with proper rules and explanations. Moreover, dictionary skills are taught in books 3 to 5.
- **Grammar:** Grade-appropriate grammar is explained with several visual models and extensive examples from the learner's immediate world. Plenty of varied exercises follow them to ensure the learner has learnt the concept well.
- **Listening and Speaking:** This section aims at developing students' listening, speaking, and overall communicative skills through a wide variety of tasks and pair/group activities. Pronunciation is also covered in this section in books 3 to 5.
- **Writing:** This well-graded section has a variety of age-appropriate creative and scaffolded writing tasks. These cover informal and formal letters, diary entries, flow charts, posters, stories, biographies, notices, reports, travelogues, character sketches, book reviews, recipes, acrostic poems, articles, and picture-based compositions.
- **Activities:** There is a fun activity accompanying each poem. Most of these activities require working collaboratively in groups or pairs. These activities are varied and cover various twenty-first century life skills.
- **Projects:** Three well-designed cross-curricular projects are provided that are linked to topics taught in that particular grade in other subjects.
- **Cross-curricular Vocabulary:** A word bank teaching cross-curricular vocabulary is included at the end of books 3 to 5. Words are classified according to different subjects and categories.

Workbooks

The Workbooks have been carefully mapped to the Coursebooks, and created with the intention of independent learning. Each Workbook has 8 comprehension passages including poems. The vocabulary and grammar sections include a quick recap of the concepts covered in the corresponding chapter of the Coursebook. The listening, speaking, and writing sections allow learners extra practice. Additional assessment papers included in the Workbooks are patterned on the Structured Assessments For Analyzing Learning (SAFAL). These offer a scope for assessing the competencies of critical thinking, inquiry-based learning, and analysis-based learning.

Literature Readers

The Literature Readers teach critical appreciation of literature through short stories, folktales, fairytales, poems and extracts from classics from the literature of different ages. A summary at the end offers a revision and understanding of the essence of the text. Literary devices are also taught along with a glossary of literary terms.

Teacher's Resource Pack

The Teacher's Resource Pack contains model lesson plans, additional worksheets, and grammar-based projects covering all the pedagogical aspects included in the Coursebooks, along with listening texts and answer keys to all exercises across Coursebooks, Workbooks, Literature Readers, and additional assessment papers.

Key to Icons

Enhanced English Alive is a multi-skill course that is closely aligned with the National Education Policy, 2020. It uses an interactive approach, cross-curricular themes, and experiential activities to build communicative competence in students. This series aims to prepare learners with the various skills outlined in the National Education Policy, 2020. These skills have been tagged appropriately with easily recognizable icons for the user's convenience. Here is the key to all the icons used in this series.

Cross-Curricular Content

- The cross-curricular approach to a topic recognizes that all subjects are interlinked. It includes contributions from several different disciplines or viewpoints for effective learning.
- All chapters have dedicated boxes teaching cross-curricular content appropriate to that class. These boxes cover the following:
  - ***Science Scan*** covers topics related to science.
  - ***Maths Magic*** covers topics related to mathematics.
  - ***Earth Speak*** covers topics related to geography and environmental studies.
  - ***Looking Back*** covers topics related to historical events and personalities.
  - ***Fact File*** covers topics related to general knowledge and awareness.
  - ***Lit Bits*** covers topics related to literature and famous literary figures.
  - ***Art and Culture*** covers topics related to art and culture.

Twenty-First Century Skills

- The twenty-first century skills ensure that today's students can thrive in an ever-changing world and can use these skills to learn constantly.
- Here are the most commonly cited twenty-first century skills in this series:

Critical Thinking — Critical Thinking

Communication — Communication Skills

Collaboration — Collaboration

Creative Thinking — Creativity

ICT — Information Communication Technology Skills or Digital Literacy

Experiential Learning

- Experiential learning is a process of learning through hands-on experience. Here, students 'learn by doing' an activity followed by reflective observation on the experience from multiple perspectives.
- This method helps learners link existing knowledge to understand new concepts and apply it to make decisions.

Art Integration

- Art Integrated Learning (AIL) is a teaching-learning model that integrates fine arts (painting, sculpture, architecture, music, and poetry), performing arts (theatre and dance), and photography with teaching new concepts.
- This provides students with an experiential and a multi-disciplinary learning experience.

Happiness Content

- Learning should be an enjoyable process for learners. It should focus on building and understanding new concepts rather than rote learning.
- Children should experience happiness through learning and awareness, active participation in class, and also in their relationships with their friends and family.

India Focus

- India Focus puts spotlight on the heritage, culture, customs, and history and geography of the Indian subcontinent.
- This provides students a deeper understanding of their homeland and creates a sense of solidarity.

Sustainable Development Goals

- The Sustainable Development Goals, adopted by the United Nations in 2015, are a collection of 17 interlinked global goals designed to achieve a better and more sustainable future for all by 2030. Here are the 17 goals:

Key Features

12 The Kite

Poem

Exploration

OBJECTIVES

In this chapter, we will:
- *read and enjoy the poem.*
- *learn about words related to wind.*
- *spot differences between pictures.*

WARM-UP

Mindfulness Activity
Be in charge!

A. Stand like a surfer. Your teacher will tell you how to! Then count till ten while taking calm breaths. Then shake your legs and stand on the other side. Do you feel all your unhappy and sad thoughts getting absorbed by the ground?

Remember to be aware of how your thoughts make you feel. Watch them and let them go.

B. Think of at least two things or people in your life that bring you happiness. Write a sentence on each.

117

Page 117

Objectives: All learning goals for the chapter listed out

Warm-up: Mindfulness activities to help train the student's mind to be involved in the present moment without getting distracted, followed by theme-based warm-ups

Comprehension: Covers factual, inferential, and extrapolative questions

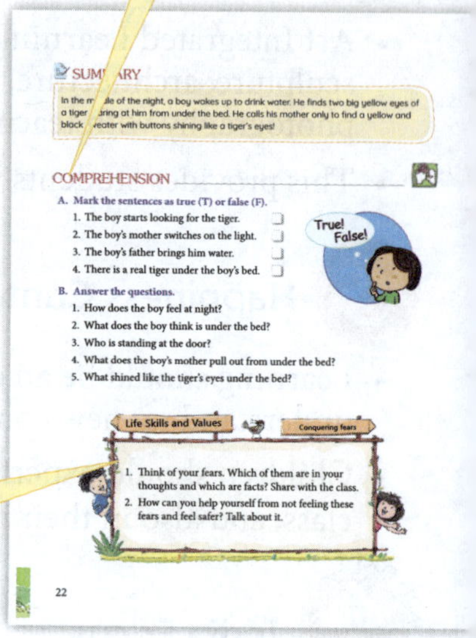

SUMMARY

In the middle of the night, a boy wakes up to drink water. He finds two big yellow eyes of a tiger staring at him from under the bed. He calls his mother only to find a yellow and black sweater with buttons shining like a tiger's eyes!

COMPREHENSION

A. Mark the sentences as true (T) or false (F).
1. The boy starts looking for the tiger.
2. The boy's mother switches on the light.
3. The boy's father brings him water.
4. There is a real tiger under the boy's bed.

B. Answer the questions.
1. How does the boy feel at night?
2. What does the boy think is under the bed?
3. Who is standing at the door?
4. What does the boy's mother pull out from under the bed?
5. What shined like the tiger's eyes under the bed?

Life Skills and Values — Conquering fears

1. Think of your fears. Which of them are in your thoughts and which are facts? Share with the class.
2. How can you help yourself from not feeling these fears and feel safer? Talk about it.

22

Page 22

Life Skills and Values: Value-based questions to develop good character through experiential learning

Reading: A good balance of Indian and global selections from a wide range of literary genres that are useful in cross-curricular teaching

Cross-curricular boxes: Topics related to other subjects highlighted

Glossary: Meanings for new words and literary devices given alongside the text

... and draw hands on the clocks.

READING

Read this poem by Eleanor Farjeon where a little girl insists to stay past her bedtime and finish everything before going to bed.

Fact File

Did you know?
- There are 60 seconds in a minute!
- 60 minutes in an hour!
- 24 hours in a day!
- 7 days in a week!
- 4 weeks in a month!
- 12 months complete a year!

castle: a large strong building, built in the past by a king/ruler for protection during wars and battles
bead-chain: Beads are small pieces of coloured glass, wood, or plastic with a hole through the middle. Beads are often put together on a piece of string or wire to make jewellery.
It's a pity: a phrase meaning it's sad

Five minutes, five minutes more, please!
Let me stay five minutes more!
Can't I just finish the castle
I'm building here on the floor?
Can't I just finish the story
I'm reading here in my book?
Can't I just finish this bead-chain —
It almost is finished, look!
Can't I just finish this game, please?
When a game's once begun
It's a pity never to find out
Whether you've lost or won.
Can't I just stay five minutes?
Well, can't I just stay just four?
Three minutes, then? two minutes?
Can't I stay one minute more?

78

Page 78

Vocabulary: Covers language skills with focus on usage

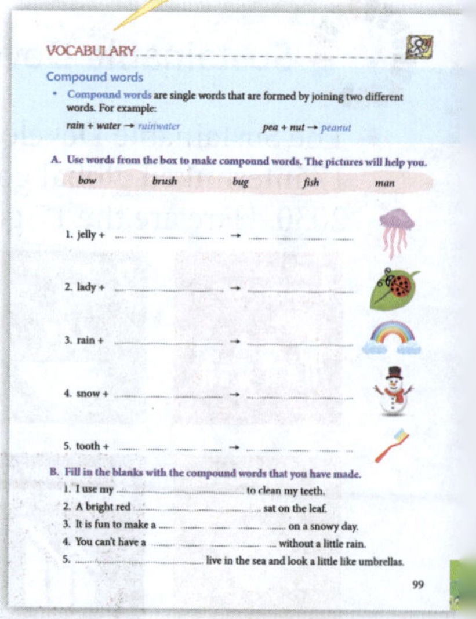

VOCABULARY

Compound words

- Compound words are single words that are formed by joining two different words. For example:

rain + water → rainwater   pea + nut → peanut

A. Use words from the box to make compound words. The pictures will help you.

bow   brush   bug   fish   man

1. jelly + ________ → ________
2. lady + ________ → ________
3. rain + ________ → ________
4. snow + ________ → ________
5. tooth + ________ → ________

B. Fill in the blanks with the compound words that you have made.
1. I use my ________ to clean my teeth.
2. A bright red ________ sat on the leaf.
3. It is fun to make a ________ on a snowy day.
4. You can't have a ________ without a little rain.
5. ________ live in the sea and look a little like umbrellas.

99

Page 99

Summary: A short summary at the end of each text for a mental revision and an easier way of remembering the essence of the text

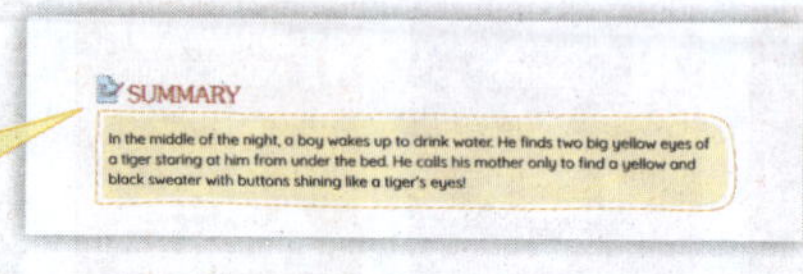

SUMMARY

In the middle of the night, a boy wakes up to drink water. He finds two big yellow eyes of a tiger staring at him from under the bed. He calls his mother only to find a yellow and black sweater with buttons shining like a tiger's eyes!

Page 22

Grammar: Grade-appropriate grammar explained with several visual models and extensive examples, followed by exercises

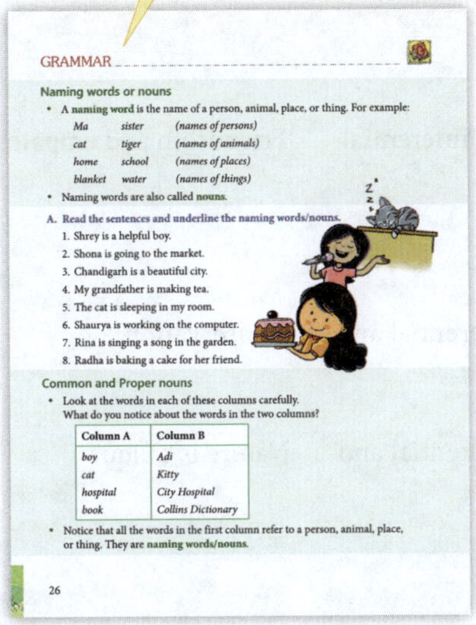

GRAMMAR

Naming words or nouns

- A naming word is the name of a person, animal, place, or thing. For example:

Ma	*sister*	*(names of persons)*
cat	*tiger*	*(names of animals)*
home	*school*	*(names of places)*
blanket	*water*	*(names of things)*

- Naming words are also called nouns.

A. Read the sentences and underline the naming words/nouns.

1. Shrey is a helpful boy.
2. Shona is going to the market.
3. Chandigarh is a beautiful city.
4. My grandfather is making tea.
5. The cat is sleeping in my room.
6. Shaurya is working on the computer.
7. Rina is singing a song in the garden.
8. Radha is baking a cake for her friend.

Common and Proper nouns

- Look at the words in each of these columns carefully. What do you notice about the words in the two columns?

Column A	Column B
boy	*Adi*
cat	*Kitty*
hospital	*City Hospital*
book	*Collins Dictionary*

- Notice that all the words in the first column refer to a person, animal, place, or thing. They are naming words/nouns.

26

Page 26

Writing: A well-graded section with a variety of creative and scaffolded writing tasks:

- letter writing
- diary entry
- flow charts
- poster making
- biography
- notice writing
- report-writing
- travelogue writing
- character sketch
- book review
- recipe writing
- acrostic poem
- description writing
- picture composition

Activity: A collaborative fun activity with each poem

ACTIVITY

Make your bedtime clock using a paper plate.

Steps:

Cut out the hands and clock face. Colour the hands of the clock as per the colour key. Use a paper fastener to attach the hands to the face. Make sure the hands turn freely. Then glue the clock face onto a paper plate. Don't forget to show your bedtime in the clock.

81

Page 81

Listening and Speaking: A wide variety of communicative activities leading to collaboration and team building; also covers pronunciation

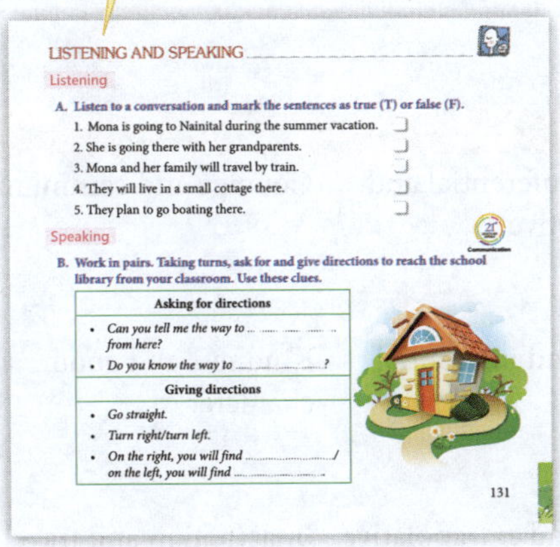

LISTENING AND SPEAKING

Listening

A. Listen to a conversation and mark the sentences as true (T) or false (F).

1. Mona is going to Nainital during the summer vacation.
2. She is going there with her grandparents.
3. Mona and her family will travel by train.
4. They will live in a small cottage there.
5. They plan to go boating there.

Speaking

B. Work in pairs. Taking turns, ask for and give directions to reach the school library from your classroom. Use these clues.

Asking for directions
• *Can you tell me the way to ______ from here?* • *Do you know the way to ______?*
Giving directions
• *Go straight.* • *Turn right/turn left.* • *On the right, you will find ______/ on the left, you will find ______.*

131

Page 131

Project: Three cross-curricular projects linked to topics taught in other subjects in this grade

PROJECT 1

Creatures of the Night

There are many animals that are active only at night.

Think of any four such animals. Work in groups of four, and gather information about them from the Internet or books. Then make a chart.

You can stick pictures of the animals on the chart paper and write down their names. Mention three interesting facts you found out about them. Decorate your chart and hang it in the classroom. Look at the sample given below.

60

Page 60

This series integrates the essence of ***NIPUN Bharat*** *guidelines and the requirements of* ***Structured Assessments For Analyzing Learning (SAFAL).***

Detailed Contents

	Vocabulary	Grammar	Listening and Speaking	Writing/Activity
	• Rhyming words			• Describing your appearance • Naming your qualities • Writing a poem about yourself using the given clues
	• Animals of the jungle • Words that express feelings • Rebus on facial expressions	• Naming words or nouns • Common and proper nouns • Capital letters, the comma and the full stop	• Listening to instructions and completing a picture • Expressing feelings in different situations	• Completing sentences on personal feelings
	• *one* (singular) and *many* (plural) • Alphabetical order	• Sentences and questions • Pronouns	• Listening to a story and filling in the blanks • Enacting a role-play on welcoming a new student to the class	• Writing about your best friend and things you like to do together
	• Names of water bodies			• Reading an imaginary dialogue • Performing a role-play on greetings
	• Words used to describe sounds	• Adjectives • Articles *a* and *an*	• Listening and sequencing sentences • Describing the physical appearance of someone you know	• Writing about a person you love
	• Words that imitate their sound			• Solving sums and colouring a picture based on the colour key
	• Words with two or more meanings	• Prepositions • The apostrophe	• Listening and marking T/F • Acting out movement words and framing sentences	• Completing a story on an animal of your choice
	• Action words			• Making a bedtime clock using a paper plate
	• Synonyms • Giving feelings to non-human things	• Simple present tense • Present continuous tense	• Listening to a description and identifying the names of animals/birds/insects • Show and tell	• Writing your daily routine using the simple present tense
	• Compound words	• Simple past tense • Past continuous tense	• Listening to a short paragraph and filling in the blanks • Describing picture postcards	• Writing an acrostic poem
	• Opposites • Homophones	• Joining words: *and* and *but* • Question mark and exclamation mark	• Listening to a story and filling in the blanks • Enacting an episode from the play	• Completing a thank-you note
	• Words related to wind			• Spotting differences between the two pictures
	• Words related to travelling • Alphabetical order of words starting with the same letter	• Using *am, is, are* • Questions with *wh-* words	• Listening to a conversation and marking T/F • Asking and giving directions using the given clues	• Writing a postcard

Contents

Poem

1 Caterpillar

Appreciating Nature

OBJECTIVES

In this chapter, we will:

- *read and understand the poem.*
- *learn and use rhyming words.*
- *learn words to describe ourselves.*
- *complete a card about ourselves.*

WARM-UP

Mindfulness Activity

Deep into nature

A. Go for a nature walk with your classmates. Look at the plants, birds, insects, trees and all the things around you. Come back to your classroom. Sit quietly. Think of the things that you saw, heard, smelt and felt. Now write two things in each column.

My nature walk	
I saw… 1. .... 2.	I heard… 1. .... 2. ....
I smelt… 1. .... 2.	I felt… 1. .... 2. ....

B. **What is this insect called? Colour the picture with the crayons you like.**

The insect is called a ....

READING

Do you know what a caterpillar turns into when it grows up? Read this poem by Christina Rossetti to find out.

Brown and furry
Caterpillar in a hurry,
Take your walk
To the shady leaf, or stalk,
Or what not,
Which may be the chosen spot.
No toad spy you,
Hovering bird of prey pass by you;
Spin and die,
To live again a butterfly.

furry: covered in thick, soft hair
stalk: the main stem of a plant
toad: a small animal that has a rough skin and lives both on land and in water
spy: to watch someone secretly
hovering: staying in one place in the air, usually by moving the wings quickly
bird of prey: a bird that eats other animals and birds

Science Scan

How are frogs and toads different?

- Frogs live near water. Toads prefer moist, open places like fields and grasslands.
- Frogs have smooth, moist skin. Toads have bumpy, rough skin.
- Frogs take long high jumps. Toads take small hops or prefer to run.

SUMMARY

The poem describes the journey of a caterpillar. The caterpillar saves herself from toads and birds, and spins her cocoon. Inside the cocoon, the caterpillar's old body dissolves and a new body is formed which comes out as a butterfly.

COMPREHENSION

Answer the questions.

1. Write two words to describe how the caterpillar looks like.
2. Where is the caterpillar going?
3. Who spies on the caterpillar in the poem?
4. Who wants to eat the caterpillar?
5. What does the caterpillar turn into?

Life Skills and Values — Nature and self

1. If you turn into a butterfly, what will you look like? What will you do? Talk about it to your friends.
2. Like the caterpillar grows from an egg into a butterfly, look at your photos or your parents' photos and see the different stages of their life. Draw how you feel you will look when you grow as old as your mother and father. Show your drawing to the class.

VOCABULARY

Rhyming words

- Words that end with the same sound are called **rhyming words**.
- Read these rhyming words aloud.

take – make	*bag – rag – tag*
spin – win	*cake – lake – rake*
brown – crown	*hug – mug – rug*

A. **Find out the words from the poem that rhyme with these words.**

1. furry ....
2. walk ....
3. not ....
4. die ....

B. **Write two rhyming words for each word.**

1. bag ....
2. feet ....
3. frog ....
4. hat ....
5. tall ....
6. tin ....

ACTIVITY

A. **The caterpillar in the poem is brown and furry. How will you describe yourself? Read the sentences. Choose the words that describe you.**

21st CENTURY SKILLS
Critical Thinking

1. I am .... (*tall/short/of medium height*).
2. I am .... (*young/old*).
3. I have .... (*long/short*) hair.
4. My hair is .... (*brown/black*).
5. I have .... (*brown/black/blue*) eyes.

B. Read these word meanings. Underline the words that describe you best.

1. brave	you don't get scared easily
2. friendly	you always smile and don't fight with your friends
3. helpful	you like to do things for other people
4. gentle	you think about another person's feelings also
5. caring	you look after animals and people

C. Now fill in this card about yourself using the words you have just underlined. You can also use other words.

....

(*Write your first name.*)

....

(*Write two words to describe yourself.*)

....

(*Write three action words that describe the things you like to do.*)

This is me!

....

(*Write your full name.*)

2 Under My Bed

Self and Imagination

OBJECTIVES

In this chapter, we will:

- *read the story of a boy who gets scared at night.*
- *learn feeling words.*
- *learn naming words, their types and punctuation marks.*
- *learn to express our feelings in different situations.*
- *write about our feelings.*

WARM-UP

Mindfulness Activity
Managing emotions

A. **Sometimes we feel happy, sad, or scared of things that do not seem real. They are from our imagination, and not facts.**

Read the following situations and mark them as fact or imagination. How do/did these situations make you feel?

Draw the face if you have a different feeling from the ones given. Colour your feeling.

Situation	Fact	Imagination	Feeling
1. The soup is so hot! After swallowing one spoonful, I can blow out fire from my mouth.			
2. I am strong. I can hit the tennis ball across the court.			

3. I went to the zoo and saw a giraffe.			
4. The lion is roaring outside my door.			
5. My mother does not love me. She refused to buy me a chocolate bar.			

Which feeling did you colour most?

Sometimes when our feelings are very strong, we find it hard to breathe easily. Then stop. Breathe in and breathe out slowly and deeply till you feel comfortable.

You can share your feelings with your family, your friends and your teachers too!

B. Work in pairs. Look at the pictures. Do you see pictures within the pictures? Take turns to tell your partner what you see.

READING

Sometimes we see strange things that are not there in reality. Read the story of a boy who sees something under his bed at night and gets scared.

Science Scan

- Tigers are the largest wild cats in the world.
- Tigers eat meat. They hunt for food at night.
- Tigers are very good swimmers and runners.

looking for: trying to find; searching for
slippers: loose soft shoes that you wear in the house

Then someone turns on the light. Ma is standing at the door.

I point towards the tiger. Ma bends and pulls the tiger out from under the bed!

turns on: switches on
point: to indicate with the finger or with something held in the hand

SUMMARY

In the middle of the night, a boy wakes up to drink water. He finds two big yellow eyes of a tiger staring at him from under the bed. He calls his mother only to find a yellow and black sweater with buttons shining like a tiger's eyes!

COMPREHENSION

A. Mark the sentences as true (T) or false (F).

1. The boy starts looking for the tiger. ☐
2. The boy's mother switches on the light. ☐
3. The boy's father brings him water. ☐
4. There is a real tiger under the boy's bed. ☐

B. Answer the questions.

1. How does the boy feel at night?
2. What does the boy think is under the bed?
3. Who is standing at the door?
4. What does the boy's mother pull out from under the bed?
5. What shined like the tiger's eyes under the bed?

Life Skills and Values

Conquering fears

1. Think of your fears. Which of them are in your thoughts and which are facts? Share with the class.
2. How can you help yourself from not feeling these fears and feel safer? Talk about it.

VOCABULARY

A. These animals are found in jungles. Read the clues and guess their names.

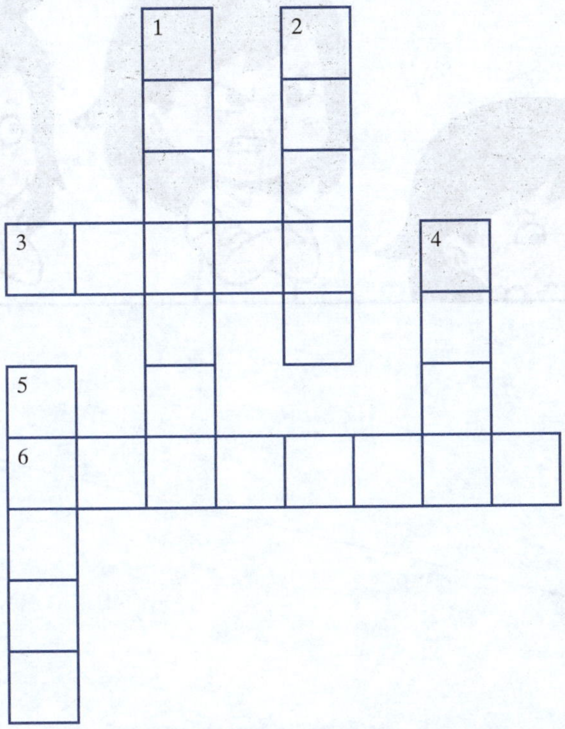

Down:

1. I have dark patches of orange or brown. I have a very long neck.
2. I am a big orange cat with black stripes. I am powerful with sharp eyes.
4. My body is orange-brown. Everyone calls me the king of the jungle.
5. I am black and white. My name starts with letter 'Z'.

Across:

3. I come in many colours. I don't have legs as I slither on the ground.
6. My colour is greyish black. I have a long trunk.

Words that express feelings

- In the story, the boy felt frightened. He also felt thirsty. *Frightened* and *thirsty* are **feeling words**.

B. Match the words with the facial expressions. One has been done for you.

21st CENTURY SKILLS
Critical Thinking

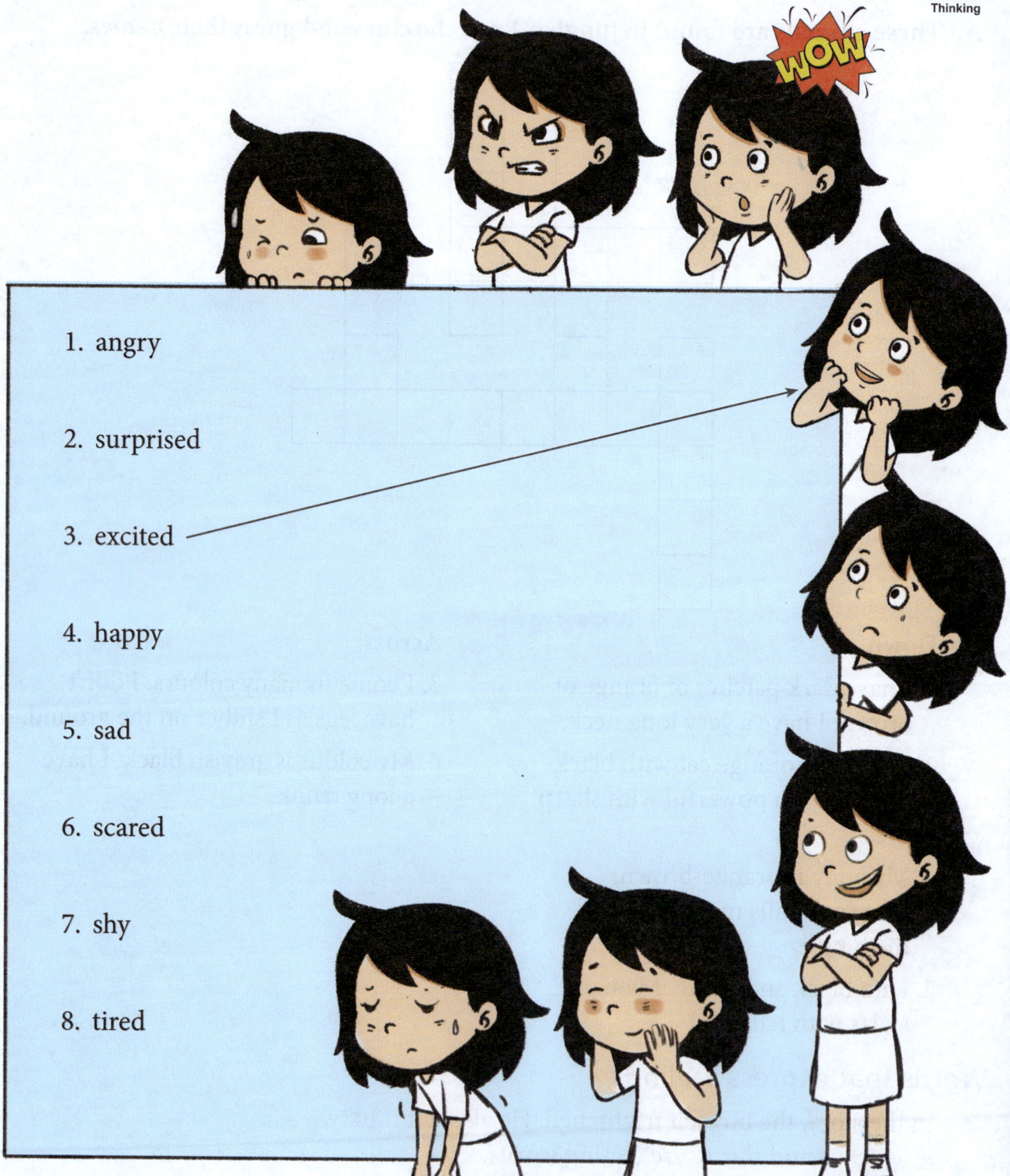

1. angry
2. surprised
3. excited
4. happy
5. sad
6. scared
7. shy
8. tired

C. Complete the story using the feeling words that you have just learned.

It was Sona's birthday. Nobody had come to wish her.

She felt .... 

She went out of her room. There was a box lying on the table.

She got ....  and opened the box.

She was .... 

to see five of her favourite storybooks.

In her excitement, Sona jumped so high that she broke a flowerpot.

She felt ....  when she thought of her mother's

....  face.

But her mother gave her a big smile and wished her a happy birthday.

Suddenly, the doorbell rang and she saw her ....  neighbour standing at the door with a cake.

Sona was ....  to see her.

They played many games together. By evening, Sona was

very ....  She went to sleep.

GRAMMAR

Naming words or nouns

- A **naming word** is the name of a person, animal, place, or thing. For example:

Ma	*sister*	*(names of persons)*
cat	*tiger*	*(names of animals)*
home	*school*	*(names of places)*
blanket	*water*	*(names of things)*

- Naming words are also called **nouns.**

A. Read the sentences and underline the naming words/nouns.

1. Shrey is a helpful boy.
2. Shona is going to the market.
3. Chandigarh is a beautiful city.
4. My grandfather is making tea.
5. The cat is sleeping in my room.
6. Shaurya is working on the computer.
7. Rina is singing a song in the garden.
8. Radha is baking a cake for her friend.

Common and Proper nouns

- Look at the words in each of these columns carefully.
What do you notice about the words in the two columns?

Column A	Column B
boy	*Adi*
cat	*Kitty*
hospital	*City Hospital*
book	*Collins Dictionary*

- Notice that all the words in the first column refer to a person, animal, place, or thing. They are **naming words/nouns.**

- The words in the second column refer to a specific person, animal, place, or thing. For example:

  Adi is a boy.

  Here, *Adi* and *boy* are naming words/nouns.

  The word *boy* is a name common to all boys.

  Adi is the name of a specific boy.
- The words in the first column are **common nouns**, as they refer to any person, place, animal, or thing.
- The words in the second column are **proper nouns**, as they refer to a specific person, place, animal, or thing.
- Common nouns do not begin with a capital letter unless they begin a sentence.
- Proper nouns always begin with a capital letter.
- Proper nouns include:
  - names of people and pets.
  - names of places (villages, cities, states, countries, and continents).
  - names of rivers, lakes, seas, oceans, and mountains.
  - names of buildings, monuments, and national parks.
  - names of languages, books, songs, and films.
  - names of the days of the week, months of the year, and festivals.

  For example:

Common noun	**Proper noun**
cities	*Jaipur, Shillong, Trichy*
countries	*India, Russia, South Africa*
monuments	*India Gate, Qutab Minar, Taj Mahal*
months	*January, February, March*
languages	*Marathi, Tamil, Urdu*
books	*Aesop's Fables, Jataka Tales, Panchatantra*
festivals	*Christmas, Eid, Holi*

B. Circle the proper nouns and underline the common nouns.

1. Joe is my brother.
2. Raju has a big dog.
3. Tina rides a bicycle.
4. Sharda plays in the park.
5. Holi is a festival of colours.
6. My birthday is in January.
7. Alia likes to read storybooks.
8. Rita and Tara are best friends.

Punctuation

- We use some special marks while writing. They are called **punctuation marks**.

Capital letter

- We always begin a sentence with a capital letter. For example:

  She is playing football.

  Raj loves to bake cakes.

- Common nouns do not begin with a capital letter if they are not the first word of a sentence. For example:

  Birds should not be caged.

  Penny is wearing a beautiful frock.

- All proper nouns begin with a capital letter. For example:

  Raj and Rishi are brothers.

  Aryan goes to his grandmother's house on Saturdays.

Comma (,)

- A **comma** (,) is a small mark used to separate words in a list. For example:

  I have a spoon, a knife, a fork, and a plate.

  He bought rice, sugar, oil, and bread.

Full stop (.)

- While writing, we put a full stop (.) at the end of a sentence that gives us some information. For example:

  I am a good student.

C. Rewrite the sentences using capital letters, commas, and full stops.

1. richa plays tennis

   ....

2. sarthak lives in kolkata

   ....

3. the qutab minar is in delhi

   ....

4. babu loves eating mangoes

   ....

5. diya has two dogs a cat and a rabbit as pets

   ....

6. please give me a diary a pen a pencil and a sharpener

   ....

7. i was busy on Monday Tuesday Wednesday and Thursday

   ....

8. i like to play hide-and-seek monopoly badminton and tennis

   ....

LISTENING AND SPEAKING

Listening

A. Look at the picture. Listen and follow the instructions carefully.

Speaking

B. Sit in a circle with your classmates. Take turns and tell your teacher how you would feel in these situations.

Communication

1. You find out that you have lost your favourite toy.
2. Your friends don't let you join in when they are playing.
3. Your art teacher holds up your drawing to show it to the class.

WRITING

Complete these sentences with words of your choice.

1. I am happy when ....
2. When I am sad, ... makes me feel better.
3. When I am hungry, I usually eat ....
4. When I get late for school, I feel ....
5. I sometimes get frightened when ....

3 No Smiles Today

Short story

Friendship

OBJECTIVES

In this chapter, we will:

- *read the story of a happy girl who suddenly stops smiling.*
- *learn singular and plural forms and write words in alphabetical order.*
- *learn about sentences and questions, pronouns and their usage.*
- *do a role-play.*
- *write about a best friend.*

WARM-UP

Mindfulness Activity
The importance of others

A. Close your eyes. Think of the person sitting next to you. Say a good thing about him/her.

Open your eyes. What did you say? Was it one of these things?

B. Look at these pictures. Draw a happy smiley under the ones that show friends you would like to be with. Draw a sad smiley under those that show friends you would not like to be with.

1.

2.

3.

4.

Who, among the above pictures, is most likely to be you? Write the picture number.

C. You like to be with people who are cheerful and pleasant, don't you? Are you smiling and pleasant at all times? Discuss these questions with your partner.

1. What reasons could be there for you to not smile sometimes?
2. Were they the same for both of you or different? Share with the class.

READING

Shanti was a happy girl. No one had ever seen her sad or quiet. Then one day, she went very quiet. What happened to Shanti? Read on to find out.

Shanti and Arun lived in the same village. They were best friends. They had a lot of fun together. They shared secrets in class. They ran races on their way home. Shanti was always cheerful.

One day, Shanti came into the classroom slowly.
Her head was bent. She looked sad.
'Did someone scold you?' asked Arun. Shanti shook her head.
She sat down and did not look up.
She did not say 'present' when the teacher called out her name.
The teacher called out again, louder this time, 'Shanti Kumari!'
Shanti raised her hand.

secrets: things known to only a few people and not told to everyone
cheerful: to look happy
scold: to speak angrily to someone because they have done something wrong
raised: lifted

Maths Magic

By the time you are 3, you have 10 teeth in the upper jaw and 10 teeth in the lower jaw.
Count and share how many milk teeth you have right now.

'Do you have a sore throat?' the teacher asked her.
Shanti shook her head.
Her cheeks were red, and it looked like she had a fever.
'Are you feeling okay?' the teacher asked.
Shanti nodded, still not daring to look up.

'Why does Shanti look so sad?' her classmates thought.
'Is your little brother okay?' one of her friends asked.
'Is your puppy okay?'
'Is your grandmother okay?'

Shanti kept nodding her head to each of her friends.
But she did not look up.

Arun wanted to make her smile. He had an idea.
He took out something from his bag.
As he ran to show it to Shanti, it slipped out of his hands.
Shanti saw something flying towards her and she grabbed it.

sore: painful
daring: brave
classmates: students who are in the same class
nodding: moving the head up and down showing understanding or agreement
grabbed: caught suddenly

It was a big green rubber frog. Shanti laughed.

Arun and other friends of Shanti saw why she had not smiled or talked all day.

Four of her front teeth had fallen.

Science Scan

- It's natural for baby teeth to fall out. Children usually start to lose teeth between ages 5 and 7.
- As children grow, milk teeth fall out. They are replaced by permanent adult teeth. So don't feel sad when your milk teeth fall off.
- Do you know when you grow up you will have 32 teeth?

SUMMARY

Arun and Shanti were best friends and had a lot of fun together. One day, Shanti looked quite sad. Everyone tried to know about her sadness but Shanti just nodded silently. Arun then tossed a green rubber frog at her, which made her laugh. The reason for her sadness was revealed — Shanti had lost four of her front teeth.

COMPREHENSION

A. Fill in the blanks.

1. Shanti was always .... (*cheerful/sad*).
2. Shanti's cheeks were .... (*red/white*), and it looked like she had a fever.
3. Arun wanted to make Shanti .... (*happy/sad*).

B. Answer the questions.

1. What did Arun and Shanti do on their way home?
2. What did Shanti do when the teacher called out her name again?
3. What did Arun take out from his bag?
4. Why had Shanti not talked or smiled all day?

Life Skills and Values | **Friendship and empathy**

1. Would you like to have a friend like Arun? Tell your class.
2. If one of your friends loses a tooth, will you laugh at him/her? Why/Why not? Discuss.

VOCABULARY

One (singular) and many (plural)

- A naming word may mean one person/thing or many persons/things.
- A word that means one person/thing is called **singular**.
- A word that means two or more persons/things is called **plural**. For example:

  one friend → *many friends*

  one frog → *three frogs*

- We add *-s* or *-es* to change a singular word into a plural word.
- Words that end in *-ch*, *-s*, *-sh*, *-ss*, *-o*, or *-x*, take *-es* to form their plural. For example:

  one bench → *six benches*

  one bus → *two buses*

  one brush → *seven brushes*

  one glass → *three glasses*

  one mango → *five mangoes*

  one box → *four boxes*

A. Change the following words into plurals. Then complete the crossword.

Across:

4. mango ....

6. insect ....

7. glass ....

Down:

1. bag ....

2. dress ....

3. sandwich ....

5. brush ....

B. Fill in each blank with the plural of the noun given in brackets.

1. The girls climbed the .... (*tree*).
2. The birds ate two .... (*bunch*) of grapes.
3. We saw many .... (*flower*) in the garden.
4. Parul placed three .... (*dish*) on the table.
5. There were three .... (*buffalo*) walking down the road.

Alphabetical order

- Read the names of body parts.

  teeth *ears* *hair* *neck* *chin* *face*

- We can write these names in alphabetical order, from a to z.
- We look at the first letter of each word to write the words alphabetically. For example:

  chin *ears* *face* *hair* *neck* *teeth*

C. Write the following words in alphabetical order.

1. bear dog cat horse

   ....

2. cake pizza burger muffin

   ....

3. table chair bed sofa

   ....

Sentences and questions

- A **sentence** is a group of words that tells us a complete thought. For example:

  Arun wanted to make her smile.

  He took out something from his bag.

- A **question** is a sentence that asks for information. For example:

  Are you feeling okay?

  Is your little brother okay?

- If a question starts with *are, is, do,* or *does*, the answer is usually *yes* or *no*.

A. Put the words in the correct order to make sentences.

1. gave I her pot a.

   ....

2. is friend a good Sarla.

   ....

3. fly birds sky the in.

   ....

4. tiger wants to he see a.

   ....

B. Write questions for the answers.

1. ....?

   Yes, he is angry.

2. ....?

   No, I don't play cricket.

3. ....?

Yes, they are friends.

4. ....?

No, they are not dancing.

Pronouns

- Read the following sentences from the story.

  Shanti and Arun were best friends. Shanti and Arun had a lot of fun together.

  Shanti and Arun shared secrets in class. Shanti and Arun ran races on their way home.

- The names *Shanti* and *Arun* are repeated in all sentences.
  It does not sound good. Now read the text again.

  Shanti and Arun were best friends. They had a lot of fun together.

  They shared secrets in class. They ran races on their way home.

  The nouns *Shanti* and *Arun* have been replaced with *they*.

- Words that replace nouns are called **pronouns**.
- Here are some pronouns:

Singular pronoun	Plural pronoun
I, you, he, she, it *For example:* *I like listening to music.* *You like to play the piano.* *He is playing with a ball.* *She is a good singer.* *It is a beautiful house.*	*we, they, you* *For example:* *We like to play tennis.* *They like to dance.* *You will get a prize.*

- The pronoun *it* is used for animals and things. For example:

  I saw a monkey. It was eating bananas.

C. Replace the nouns with the pronouns *I, you, he, she, we,* or *they* and rewrite the sentences.

1. Nadia is flying a kite.

....

2. Children like to play.

....

3. Grandfather wakes up early.

....

4. Bottles are usually made of glass or plastic.

....

5. Parul and Tina are going to school.

....

D. Fill in the blanks with the pronouns *I, you, he, she, it, we,* or *they*.

1. Toby is a cute cat. .... loves to drink milk.

2. My friends and I love football. .... play football every day.

3. Sana loves watermelon.

....
ate half of it.

4. Where is Jagveer?

Is ....
in the class?

LISTENING AND SPEAKING

Listening

A. Listen to a story and choose the correct word for each blank.

1. The children went to play in the .... (*garden/park*).
2. The puppy was lying on a pile of .... (*grass/leaves*).
3. The puppy was .... (*hungry/thirsty*).
4. Siya brought .... (*milk/water*) and bread for the puppy.
5. Rohan got a warm .... (*blanket/sweater*) for the puppy.

Speaking

21st CENTURY SKILLS
Communication

B. Work in pairs. Discuss and role-play the following situation.

A new student has joined your class. How will you make him/her comfortable in school? You can talk about these things:

1. Likes and dislikes, family, favourite games, and so on
2. Tell him/her about yourself, school and teachers

WRITING

Write about your best friend. Mention two or three things you like to do together. You may choose from the given phrases.

go to park *play indoor games* *play hide-and-seek* *tell stories to each other* *solve puzzles together* *help each other with homework*

My best friend's name is ....

He/She is .... *years old.*

When we are together, we like to..

....

....

....

....

....

Poem

4 Hello! Hello!

Friendship

OBJECTIVES

In this chapter, we will:

- *read and understand the poem.*
- *learn names of water bodies.*
- *read, write and perform role-plays.*

WARM-UP

Mindfulness Activity
Mindful listening

A. **Sit in a circle. You are going to listen to the sound of the bell. When you hear the bell, focus on the sound alone. Try to listen to it until the sound fades away completely. When you can't hear it anymore (and you must be really quiet and still to hear it that long!), open your eyes. How do you feel?**

B. Help the frog reach his friend sitting on the lily-pad in the pond.

READING

Do you think animals also have fun? Read this poem by Louisa May Alcott and find out how frogs play.

Hello! hello!
Come down below—
It's lovely and cool
Out here in the pool;
On a lily-pad float
For a nice green boat.
Here we sit and sing
In a pleasant ring;
Or leap frog play,
In the jolliest way.
Our games have begun,
Come join in the fun.

pool: a small area of still water; a pond
lily-pad: (here) a floating leaf of a lily
pleasant: enjoyable or pleasing
leap: to jump high or a long way
jolliest: happiest

SUMMARY

It is a happy poem about frogs having fun in the pond. The frogs are inviting everyone into the pond where they sit and sing, and play many games.

COMPREHENSION

A. Mark the sentences as true (T) or false (F).

1. The frogs are in the pool. ☐
2. The frogs sit on the lily-pad. ☐
3. The frogs are very sad. ☐
4. The frogs are inviting everyone to come and play with them. ☐

B. Answer the questions.

1. Where is it lovely and cool?
2. What are the frogs calling a nice green boat?
3. How do the frogs play leap frog?
4. What has begun?
5. Do you feel happy or sad while reading the poem? Give reasons for your answer.

Life Skills and Values — Conservation

1. Do you think our towns and cities should have more ponds and rivers? Why/Why not? Discuss in class.
2. How can we save water every day? Think and share at least two ways.

VOCABULARY

A. Read the clues and write the names of water bodies in the crossword.

Across

3. A flowing stream of water
5. A very large body of sea water

Down

1. A place where water comes from the ground
2. A large area of water surrounded by land
4. A small area of water, usually made artificially

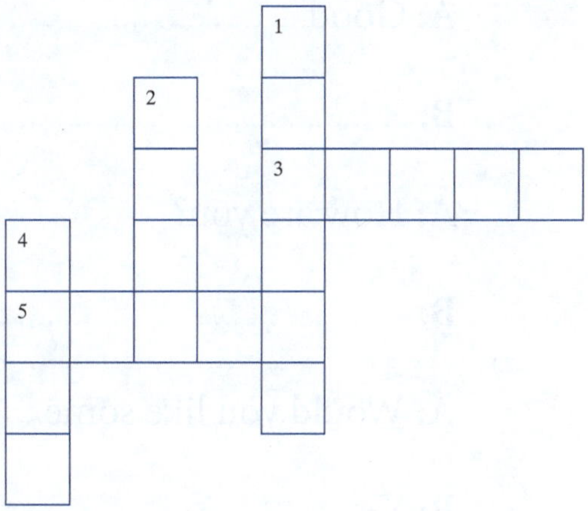

B. Use the words from the crossword to complete the sentences.

1. There are many boats on the banks of the .... Ganges.
2. We are going for picnic to Sukhna .... in Chandigarh.
3. When we went to the mountains, we saw a ....
4. In our school there is a small .... which has many fishes.
5. Whales live in the ....

ACTIVITY

A. Imagine the frog in the poem is expecting a guest. How will the frog greet his friend? Read the dialogue.

Frog: Croak! Croak! Good morning!

Friend: Croak! Croak! Good morning!

Frog: How are you?

Friend: I am well! Thank you!

Frog: Please jump into the pool. We will have lots of fun!

Friend: I will do so gladly. Thank you!

B. **Imagine your friend comes to your house. How will you greet your friend? What will you talk to him/her about? Complete the dialogue and enact it in front of your classmates.**

21st CENTURY SKILLS Communication

A: Good ....!

B: ....!

A: How are you?

B: ....

A: Would you like some ....?

B: Yes. ....

A: Let's play ....

B: Yes, of course!

5 Goodnight, Tinku!

Nature and Animals

OBJECTIVES

In this chapter, we will:

- *read the story of a pup who lives on a farm.*
- *learn to use words that describe sounds.*
- *learn adjectives and the articles a and an.*
- *listen and sequence events.*
- *describe how people look.*
- *write about people we love.*

WARM-UP

Mindfulness Activity
Relaxation practice

A. Close your eyes. Squeeze the muscles of your shoulders for ten seconds. Then relax. Next, squeeze your stomach muscles for ten seconds. Then relax. Go on and relax different muscles of your body in the same way...

Now, open your eyes. Do you feel relaxed and better? If yes, you're all set to do the next exercise.

B. Look at these animals. You will hear the sounds they make. Number them in the order in which you hear them.

C. Look at these pictures and write their names.

1. .... 2. .... 3. .... 4. ....

5. .... 6. .... 7. .... 8. ....

D. Which of the things you named can be seen during the day, during the night, or both during the day and the night? Write down their numbers in the correct circles.

21st CENTURY SKILLS Critical Thinking

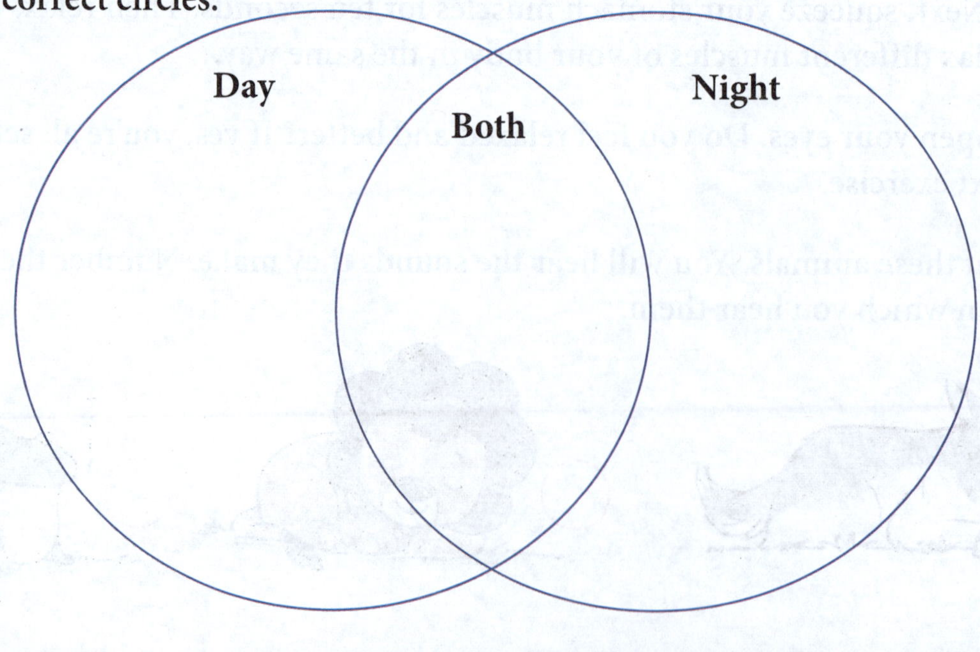

Tinku, a little pup, is not sleepy at all. He decides to go out in the night. Read on to find out what happens next.

bright: shining
moonlit: lit by the moon; full of light from the moon
murmured: said in a soft quiet voice that is difficult to hear or understand
fast asleep: in deep sleep
belly: the part of the body below the chest
set off: began a journey; started
glow: to produce a dull steady light; to shine

It was a bright moonlit night.
All the animals on Mangu's farm were sleeping.
Except Tinku!

'I am not sleepy, Ma,' murmured Tinku.
But Ma did not hear him.
She was fast asleep.

He turned left, and he turned right.
He lay on his belly, and rolled on his back.
But he could not sleep.

So he set off to see what he could find.
Up in the sky, Tinku saw the moon,
white and round, smiling down at him.
He felt very happy.

'Night is beautiful,' thought Tinku.

Far away on the top of a tree, there were some tiny lights.
One light flew down!

'I'm a firefly,' said the light. 'I glow in the dark.'
'Will you be my friend?' asked Tinku.
'Yes, I will!' said the firefly.

Something flew by and hung upside down on a tree.
'What is your name, bird?' asked Tinku.
'I am not a bird. I am a bat. I can see at night!' said the bat.

'Will you be my friend?' asked Tinku.

'Yes, I will!' said the bat.

A few leaves moved in the bushes. Someone was hiding there.

'Who are you?' asked Tinku.

'I am a fox,' said the fox. 'I go strolling in the night.'

'Will you be my friend?' asked Tinku.

'Yes, I will!' said the fox.

Two shiny eyes looked at him from a tree.

'Who are you?' asked Tinku.

'I am an owl,' said the owl. 'I hunt for food during the night.'

'Will you be my friend?' asked Tinku.

'Yes, I will!' said the owl.

'Chirrrrrp! Chirrrrrp!'

'Who is there?' Tinku asked.

'I'm a cricket,' said the cricket. 'I chirp when it is dark.'

'Will you be my friend?' asked Tinku.

'Yes, I will!' said the cricket.

Tinku and his friends jumped and tossed and rolled until Tinku felt sleepy. 'I am sleepy. I have to go home now,' said Tinku. He was happy that he had many new friends.

Snuggling close to Ma, he said, 'Night is not a bad time, Ma. It is full of wonderful beings.'

'Yes!' replied Ma. 'Your new friends are nocturnal, just like wild dogs.'

'Nocturnal animals eat, play and work at night. They rest during the day. You must sleep now. Sleep will give you

Science Scan

- Bats are not birds; they are animals with wings.
- Bats do not lay eggs but give birth to babies.
- They feed their milk to their babies.

strolling: walking in a slow, relaxed manner
tossed: moved from side to side
snuggling: getting in a comfortable position and close to somebody
nocturnal: active at night

energy to play with your daytime friends tomorrow. Goodnight, dear!' she said, hugging him tight.

The bright round moon shone all night, spreading her light all around. And Tinku slept all through the night.

SUMMARY

The little pup, Tinku, could not sleep one night so he decides to go for a walk. He makes friends with many nocturnal animals like the firefly, the bat, the fox, the owl and the cricket. They all play together till Tinku feels sleepy, and decides to return home.

energy: the ability to put effort in an activity; strength

COMPREHENSION

A. Mark the sentences as true (T) or false (F).

1. All the animals on Mangu's farm were playing. ☐
2. Tinku was not sleepy. ☐
3. The bat cannot see at night. ☐
4. The owl hunts for food at night. ☐
5. Crickets chirp at night. ☐
6. Nocturnal animals eat and play during the day. ☐

B. Answer the questions.

1. Who was Tinku? Where did Tinku live?
2. What was the *light* that flew down?
3. What was hanging upside down?
4. What was the fox doing?
5. Why was Tinku happy at the end of his trip?
6. What are nocturnal animals?

Life Skills and Values

Nature is unique

1. Have you ever seen nocturnal animals or heard their sounds? Describe them.
2. Research and find out why people are not allowed to visit national parks at night. Share your findings.

VOCABULARY

Words used to describe sounds

- Some words describe sounds.
- In the story, Tinku murmurs to his mother and the cricket chirps. The words *murmur* and *chirp* describe sounds.
- Look at some more examples.

  The bell rings. *The tiger roars.*

  The owl hoots. *The boy screams.*

Fill in each blank with the right word from the box.

boom *buzzing* *meow* *tick-tock* *whisper* *zoomed*

1. The cars .... past us.
2. I want to .... a secret into your ear.
3. The bees were .... around the flowers.
4. The .... of the clock could be heard all night.
5. Shreya could hear the cat's .... from the house.
6. The loud .... of the firecrackers scared the dogs.

GRAMMAR

Adjectives

- Words that tell us something about people, places, things and animals are called **describing words** or **adjectives**. For example:

  There were some tiny lights.

  The bright round moon shone all night.

  Nocturnal animals eat, play, and work at night.

  The word *tiny* tells us the size of the lights.

  The words *bright* and *round* describe the moon.

  The word *nocturnal* tells us about the kind of animals.

- Here are some more examples:

  Zaid plays with a red ball.

  The giraffe has a long neck.

  The furry cat is sitting under the big bed.

A. Look at the picture and fill in the blanks with the words given in brackets.

1. There is a ladder kept outside the .... (*big/small*) hut.
2. There are .... (*green/red*) trees behind the small hut.
3. The roof of the huts is made of .... (*black/yellow*) hay.
4. A .... (*large/little*) cat is sleeping on the mama cow.
5. The .... (*round/square*) and .... (*black/white*) moon is smiling down.

B. Look at the pictures and write two adjectives to describe each picture. One has been done for you.

1.  apple ....*juicy*........ ....*red*........

2.  book ....

3.  cake ....

4.  car ....

5.  elephant ....

Articles

- The words *a* and *an* are called **articles**.
- We use *a* and *an* before naming words or nouns that can be counted and are just one in number. For example:

  I am a fox.

  My sister and her friends play with a ball.

  There is an ice cream in the fridge.

  I can see an elephant eating leaves from a tree.
- We don't use *a* and *an* with nouns that are more than one in number.

  Girls are playing badminton.
- We don't use *a* and *an* before nouns that cannot be counted. For example:

  Milk is good for our health.
- We use *an* before words that begin with a vowel sound (a, e, i, o, u). For example:

  an apple *an egg* *an igloo* *an orange* *an umbrella*
- We use *a* before words that begin with consonant sounds. For example:

  a ball *a cat* *a dog* *a firefly* *a zoo*

C. Write *a* or *an*. Put a cross (X) for the nouns that cannot be counted.

1. .... air
2. .... doctor
3. .... egg
4. .... milk
5. .... night
6. .... officer

D. Fill in the blanks with *a* or *an*. Put a cross (X) where no article is required.

Rajesh is .... firefighter. He puts out .... fires with .... water. He uses .... water hose. Rajesh rides .... fire truck.

One day Rajesh got .... phone call from John. John and Rajesh are .... friends. John told Rajesh that .... cat was stuck in .... tree. He wanted Rajesh to help him. Rajesh went to John's house. He took out .... ladder from his fire truck and climbed the tree. He gave the cat .... egg to eat and easily brought him down.

LISTENING AND SPEAKING

Listening

A. Listen to the story carefully and number the sentences in the correct order.

1. The dog hid behind the hut. ☐
2. A dog was sleeping under a tree. ☐
3. One day the sun was shining brightly. ☐
4. The bear looked around and then went back to the jungle. ☐
5. The hen saw a big bear from the tree and shouted, 'Bear! Bear!' ☐

Speaking

21st CENTURY SKILLS Critical Thinking

B. Work in pairs. Describe the physical appearance of someone you know to your partner. You may talk about a family member or a classmate. Include the following points in the description:

- *body build (tall, short, thin, etc.)*
- *face shape (oval, round, triangular, etc.)*
- *eyes (size and colour)*
- *hair (colour and length)*
- *kind of clothes the person usually wears*

WRITING

Write a few lines about a person you love wholeheartedly. Mention what you like about him/her. Follow these steps.

- Start by naming the person.
  I love...
- What are the things you like to do with that person?
  Read a book, play a game, talk about adventures...
- How do you take care of that person?
  I help the person clean/cook/do homework...
- What are the things/qualities you love about the person?
  I love him/her because...

PROJECT 1

Critical Thinking

Creatures of the Night

There are many animals that are active only at night.

Think of any four such animals. Work in groups of four, and gather information about them from the Internet or books. Then make a chart.

You can stick pictures of the animals on the chart paper and write down their names. Mention three interesting facts you found out about them. Decorate your chart and hang it in the classroom. Look at the sample given below.

Creatures of the night

Place image of animal here	Place image of animal here	Place image of animal here	Place image of animal here
1..............................	2..............................	3..............................	4..............................

Interesting facts

1. ....
   ....
2. ....
   ....
3. ....
   ....

1. ....
   ....
2. ....
   ....
3. ....
   ....

1. ....
   ....
2. ....
   ....
3. ....
   ....

1. ....
   ....
2. ....
   ....
3. ....
   ....

6 The Cow

Respecting Nature

OBJECTIVES

In this chapter, we will:

- *read and understand the poem.*
- *learn words that imitate animal sounds.*
- *perform a fun activity and colour a picture.*

WARM-UP

Mindfulness Activity
Imagination

A. Close your eyes. Imagine yourself as a farm animal wandering through the vast open fields. What would be your day like? Open your eyes and draw pictures of the things you would enjoy doing. Show your drawing to the class.

B. What do these farm animals give us? Trace and find out.

21st CENTURY SKILLS Critical Thinking

READING

The poet, Robert Louis Stevenson, tells us about a cow who loves to roam around in peace and be happy. Let's read the poem to find out more.

The friendly cow all red and white,
I love with all my heart;
She gives me cream with all her might,
To eat with apple tart.
She wanders lowing here and there,
And yet she cannot stray,
All in the pleasant open air,
The pleasant light of day;
And blown by all the winds that pass
And wet with all the showers,
She walks among the meadow grass
And eats the meadow flowers.

might: strength
apple tart: a sweet dish; a pastry made with apples
wanders: walks around without purpose
lowing: the sound made by a cow
stray: to move here and there
showers: brief and light fall of rain
meadow: a field which has grass and flowers growing in it

SUMMARY

The poet talks about his cow. He enjoys his dessert of apple tart with the cream he gets from the cow. The poet then describes the way the cow spends her time wandering in vast green fields, enjoying the wind, the rain and flowers.

COMPREHENSION

A. Choose the correct option.

1. In the poem, the colour of the cow is
   a. red and black.
   b. red and white.
   c. black and white.
2. *She gives me milk with all her might* means
   a. the cow gives milk happily.
   b. the cow is forced to give milk.
   c. the cow puts lots of strength in giving milk.
3. In the poem, the cow eats
   a. the meadow hay.
   b. the meadow grass.
   c. the meadow flowers.

B. Answer the questions.

1. How does the poet feel about the cow?
2. What does the cow give the poet? What does the poet eat it with?
3. Where does the cow wander?
4. What does the cow do while she wanders?
5. *She wanders lowing here and there,*
   And yet she cannot stray
   a. Do you think the cow can roam around as she wishes?
   b. What do you think the cow cannot do?

Life Skills and Values

Empathy with animals

1. Do you think we should be kind towards only those animals who give us something in return? Why/Why not? Discuss in class.
2. There are many animals on the street. Suggest ways in which we can take care of street animals.

VOCABULARY

Words that imitate their sound

- Read this line from the poem.

  She wanders lowing here and there.

  The word *lowing* describes the sound cows make.
- The word *moo* also describes the sound cows make.
- The words *lowing* and *moo* imitate the sounds cows make.
- Here are a few more examples:

Animal	Word that imitates its sound
cat	*mews*
wolf	*howls*
mouse	*squeaks*

A. Match the animals in Column A with the sounds they make in Column B.

Column A	Column B
1. bee	a. baa, bleat
2. dog	b. bark
3. duck	c. buzz
4. hen	d. cluck
5. horse	e. hiss
6. sheep	f. neigh
7. snake	g. quack

B. **Do the words in Column B imitate the sounds of animals? Read them aloud and find out.**

ACTIVITY

Critical Thinking

Solve the sums. Then look at the colour key and colour the picture.

0 → grey

1 → black

2 → blue

3 → green

7 Tyltyl's Adventure

Courage and Adventure

OBJECTIVES

In this chapter, we will:

- *read the story of a sea turtle.*
- *learn to use words with two or more meanings.*
- *learn to use prepositions and the apostrophe.*
- *act out and guess the word.*
- *write a story about an animal.*

WARM-UP

Mindfulness Activity
Mindful decision-making

A. Close your eyes. Think of the animals, birds and insects you see around you. Which are the ones that come to your mind? Note them. What would you like to do/feel like doing when you see them?

Now, open your eyes. Tick (✓) one of the two options given below or add one of your own.

1. It is summertime and birds are thirsty. You will
   - ☐ do nothing.
   - ☐ keep a birdfeeder with food and water outside.

2. You see a tortoise at the beach. You will
   - ☐ touch and poke it with a stick.
   - ☐ enjoy looking at its movements as it swims into the sea.

3. The garden that you often go to has so many butterflies! You will
   - ☐ chase them and try to catch them.
   - ☐ enjoy watching them as they go from one flower to another.

4. You see cows on your street feeding on garbage and plastic. You will
   - ☐ report to the authority.
   - ☐ get together with your friends and clean the area yourself to set an example for others.

5. You hear the stray dogs in your area barking on a chilly night. You will
   - ☐ ask the adults in the locality to arrange for warm dog clothes.
   - ☐ forget all about it the next morning.

B. Fill in the blanks with names of movements for each of the animals.

crawl *fly* *hop* *slither* *swim* *trot*

1. .... 2. .... 3. ....

4. .... 5. .... 6. ....

READING

A mother turtle laid some eggs on the seashore. The eggs hatched and baby turtles crawled out. One of the babies is Tyltyl who leads his brothers and sisters towards the sea. On their way, many adventures happen – some exciting, some dangerous! Read the story to know what happened to the baby turtles.

It was a bright and sunny day. The sunbeams fell on the seashore. They touched the dancing waves. They fell on the fishermen taking out their boats. They fell on the sand heap by the rocks.

The sunbeams made the sand very warm. Suddenly something moved and wriggled under it.

A tiny creature with a soft shell on its back crawled out of the sand. It was Tyltyl, the baby sea turtle.

Tyltyl was Topsy's baby. Topsy lived in the sea. But the sea is a restless place to live in. So, when it was time for her to lay eggs, she swam back to the shore. She crawled along the sand looking for a quiet place till she found a lovely corner by the rocks.

Topsy laid her eggs, buried them in the sand and swam back to the sea. The sun warmed the sand and kept the eggs warm until it was time for the baby turtles to come out. The eggs cracked and the turtle babies crawled out of the sand.

Tyltyl craned his tiny neck and looked about him. Bright sunlight shone into his eyes making him feel dizzy for a moment. He heard the roar of the sea and the sound of waves breaking over the sand. The sea was calling him!

Five more baby turtles crawled out of the sand. They were his brothers and sisters.

'Hello!' they said looking at Tyltyl.

'Hello!' replied Tyltyl, 'Come, follow me. We don't have much time.'

Science Scan

- A female sea turtle lays almost 150 eggs every two or three years.
- Sea turtles' eggs look like ping pong balls.
- Sea turtles have excellent eyesight and sense of smell.
- Sea turtles can live up to 80 years.

sunbeams: rays of the sun
heap: an untidy pile
wriggled: moved twisting and turning quickly
restless: (here) the water in the sea is always moving
buried: covered completely in sand
craned: stretched out (the neck)
dizzy: a feeling that everything is turning around and you are going to fall

'Where are we going?' asked one of them.

'To the sea, of course,' said Tyltyl.

Tyltyl led the little group across the sand. A few more turtle babies joined them. Topsy had laid nearly fifty eggs. But some of them did not get enough warmth from the sand. So they were not ready to come out. Some others had been dug up by a naughty boy who took them home.

'Keep by the rocks,' warned Tyltyl. 'Look at those big seabirds flying above. They look very bad! I hope they don't attack us.'

Before Tyltyl could finish speaking, one of the birds swooped down on them. 'Get inside your shells! Quick!' cried Tyltyl. But it was too late. A seagull grabbed one of them and flew away. They felt very sad.

'Just be careful, all of you,' said Tyltyl.

'How far is the sea?' asked one of his brothers.

'I'm hungry and thirsty too,' said another.

'There are some tiny worms here,' said Tyltyl, sniffing inside a sand heap, 'And there's water in that puddle.'

'How far is the sea?' asked a sister of Tyltyl.

'Not too far, I guess,' replied Tyltyl.

'I hope there are no more killer birds,' said the youngest of the group.

They crawled along slowly. A group of seagulls tried to get at them once more. But this time they quickly got inside their shells.

The sound of the sea grew louder. The sand beneath their feet felt wetter.

swooped: came down suddenly to attack
seagull: a bird with long wings that lives near the sea
sniffing: smelling
puddle: a small amount of water collected at a place
killer: a person or animal that kills

They were in the water now. But they were not fully safe yet. There came a shoal of big fish looking at them hungrily. 'Hide under those shells! Quick!' cried Tyltyl.

They ducked under a pile of empty shells just in time. Tyltyl looked around anxiously.

'Life seems to be hard,' said one of his brothers. 'It seems to me that we are always hiding from killers of one kind or another!'

'Life is an adventure, silly!' said Tyltyl. 'We'll all get used to it in time. And enjoy it too.'

The big fish were all gone after a while. The water looked blue. It felt as soft as silk. The sound of waves produced music. 'All clear now,' said Tyltyl in a happy voice. 'We have reached home!'

shoal: a group (of fish)
ducked: bent down
anxiously: in a worried manner
adventure: an unusual, exciting and dangerous activity

SUMMARY

Topsy, the mother turtle lays eggs in the sand. Once the eggs hatch, Tyltyl and other baby turtles start their journey towards the sea. On the way, they are attacked by a seagull who takes one of the turtles away. When they are hungry, they eat worms out of sand and drink water from a puddle, but keep moving. When the turtles are in water, a group of big fish attack them but they escape. The little turtles soon realise that life is an adventure.

COMPREHENSION

A. Mark the sentences as true (T) or false (F).

1. Topsy laid her eggs, buried them in the sand and swam back to the sea. ☐
2. Tyltyl had only two brothers and sisters. ☐
3. Tyltyl led the other baby sea turtles to the sea. ☐

4. The seagulls picked up two turtles. ☐
5. The sea turtles saved themselves from the seagulls by hiding inside their shells. ☐

B. Answer the questions.

1. How many eggs did Topsy lay?
2. Where did Topsy lay her eggs?
3. What kept the eggs warm?
4. Who was Tyltyl?
5. What did Tyltyl hear when he came out of the egg?
6. When did Tyltyl feel dizzy?
7. Why did Tyltyl tell the sea turtles to keep by the rocks?
8. What was the danger in the sea?

Life Skills and Values — Thoughtfulness and courage

1. Do you think the boy did the right thing by digging up the eggs and taking them home? Why/Why not? Share your thoughts.
2. What are some of the 'dangers' that you feel in your life? By looking at them as an adventure like Tyltyl, how would you deal with your 'dangers'?

VOCABULARY

Words with two or more meanings

- Many words in English have two or more meanings.
  For example:

  Tyltyl craned his tiny neck.

  Cranes usually fly in groups.

  In the first sentence, *crane* means *to stretch out the neck.*

  In the second sentence, *cranes* are *types of birds.*

A *crane* is also *a tall machine with a long arm used to lift and move very heavy things.*

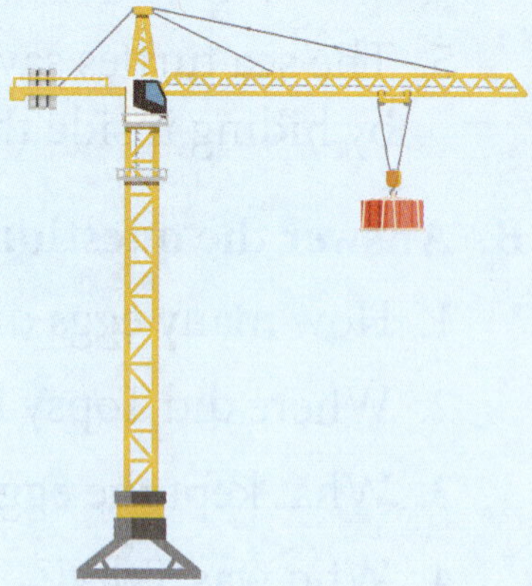

- Here is another example:

  They ducked under a pile of empty shells just in time.

  I saw a duck near the pond.

In the first sentence, *duck* means *to bend down.*

Duck is also *the name of a bird.*

A. Read the following words. One meaning of the word is given. Find and match the second meaning.

Word	Meaning 1	Meaning 2
1. bark	the sound a dog makes	to move one's hand side to side
2. bat	an animal with wings	a circular band
3. can	to be able to	a container
4. light	a lamp	the outer covering of a tree
5. play	to do things for pleasure, as a child	a type of small clock worn on the wrist
6. ring	the sound of a bell	a drama
7. watch	to look carefully	a piece of wood with a handle used to play cricket
8. wave	a raised line of water	easy to lift/not heavy

B. Read the sentences. Check the table under Exercise A and tick the correct meaning.

1. He looked at his watch and realised that he was late for school.
   a. Meaning 1 b. Meaning 2
2. When the bell rings, the children run to the playground.
   a. Meaning 1 b. Meaning 2
3. He filled the can with water and took it home.
   a. Meaning 1 b. Meaning 2
4. He heard the dogs bark all night.
   a. Meaning 1 b. Meaning 2
5. The bat was feeding milk to its baby.
   a. Meaning 1 b. Meaning 2
6. She waved goodbye to her friends.
   a. Meaning 1 b. Meaning 2
7. The bag is very light; I can carry it easily.
   a. Meaning 1 b. Meaning 2
8. The class presented a play on the stage.
   a. Meaning 1 b. Meaning 2

GRAMMAR

Prepositions

- A **preposition** connects a noun or pronoun to other words in a sentence and shows the relationship between them.
- Some prepositions show where something is. For example:

  Topsy lived in the sea.
  Tyltyl led the little group across the sand.

  Where did Topsy live? *In* the sea.
  Where did Tyltyl lead the little group? *Across* the sand.

- *In* shows a relation between the sea and Topsy. Topsy lived inside the sea.
- *Across* shows a relation between sand and Tyltyl.

- Here are some more examples:

  The book is on the table.
  The clothes are in the cupboard.
  The garden is behind the house.

- Some more prepositions are:

on above over in front of beside below under behind

A. Look at the picture carefully and fill in the correct prepositions.

1. The cat is .... (*in/on*) the roof.
2. The girl is .... (*in/on*) the house.
3. The car is .... (*behind/beside*) the house.
4. The dog is .... (*in front of/under*) the house.
5. The cow is standing .... (*behind/inside*) the house.
6. The cat is standing .... (*beside/under*) the chimney.

Apostrophe (')

- An **apostrophe** (') is a small punctuation mark used to show that something belongs to somebody. For example:

  Tyltyl was Topsy's baby.

  In the above sentence, the apostrophe shows that the *baby Tyltyl* belongs to *Topsy*.

- Here are some more examples:

  Tina's school bag is beautiful. (The school bag belongs to Tina.)

  Raj's bat is heavy. (The bat belongs to Raj.)

  My grandmother's house is very big. (The house belongs to my grandmother.)

B. Put the missing apostrophe (') in each sentence.

1. Your cats tail is short.
2. Ratnas son is in school.
3. Zoyas brother is kind.
4. Bobbys rabbit eats carrots.
5. My sisters shoes are white.
6. The elephants trunk is long.
7. Mitas bicycle is under the tree.
8. Aryas lunch box was lost yesterday.

LISTENING AND SPEAKING

Listening

A. Listen to a passage carefully. Then mark the sentences as true (T) or false (F).

1. Meera went to the beach in the morning. ☐
2. She found some empty shells lying on the sand. ☐
3. She did not pick up any shells. ☐
4. Some seagulls flew over Meera's head. ☐
5. The seagulls did not harm Meera. ☐

Speaking

21st CENTURY SKILLS Collaboration

B. Work in groups of ten. Write the words given below on separate chits. One student in the group picks up a chit and acts out the movement. The other members guess the name of the animal and the word for the movement. Each group must also say a sentence using the word.

crawl *flutter* *fly* *gallop* *hop* *jump*
prowl *slither* *trot* *waddle*

WRITING

Think of any animal. Then complete these sentences to write a story about it.

One day I went to the garden. I saw ....

(name of your animal). *It was* ....

(describe the animal). *At first I was very scared but* ....

(name of the animal) *was harmless and gentle. I took it home. I gave it* ....

.... (name of food) *to eat and* ....

.... *to drink. I named it* ....

(name given to the animal). *We became friends.*

Poem

8 Bedtime

Routine and Habits

OBJECTIVES

In this chapter, we will:

- *read the poem and talk about bedtime routine.*
- *learn about action words and use them in sentences.*
- *make a bedtime clock.*

WARM-UP

Mindfulness Activity
Gratitude practice

A. Imagine you are in front of a birthday cake with candles. Close your eyes and blow out each candle. Each time, hold your breath, think of a good thing that happened to you during the day, and breathe all the way out. Open your eyes. How do you feel?

B. Look at this empty jar. Draw something in it that you might want to see in your happy dream.
Write down two sentences on what you drew. Then tell your friends about your happy dream.

....

....

....

....

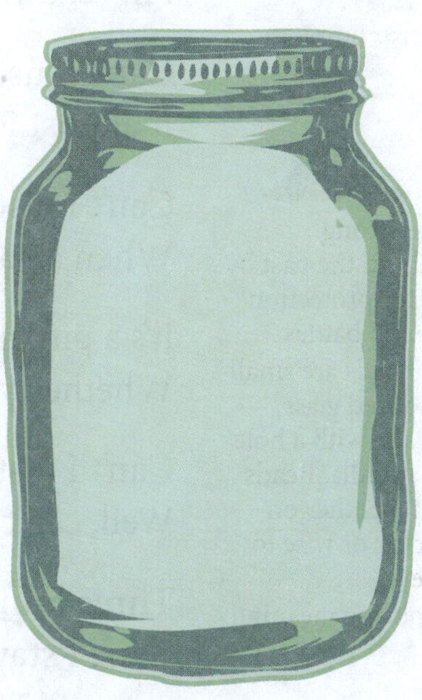

C. Look at the time and draw hands on the clocks.

READING

Read this poem by Eleanor Farjeon where a little girl insists to stay past her bedtime and finish everything before going to bed.

Fact File

Did you know?

- There are 60 seconds in a minute!
- 60 minutes in an hour!
- 24 hours in a day!
- 7 days in a week!
- 4 weeks in a month!
- 12 months complete a year!

Five minutes, five minutes more, please!
Let me stay five minutes more!

Can't I just finish the castle
I'm building here on the floor?

Can't I just finish the story
I'm reading here in my book?

Can't I just finish this bead-chain —
It almost is finished, look!

Can't I just finish this game, please?
When a game's once begun

It's a pity never to find out
Whether you've lost or won.

Can't I just stay five minutes?
Well, can't I just stay just four?

Three minutes, then? two minutes?
Can't I stay one minute more?

castle: a large strong building, built in the past by a king/ruler for protection during wars and battles
bead-chain: Beads are small pieces of coloured glass, wood, or plastic with a hole through the middle. Beads are often put together on a piece of string or wire to make jewellery.
It's a pity: a phrase meaning *it's sad*

SUMMARY

The poem is about a child who wants to stay up past her bedtime and tries to persuade her parents to let her do so. She wants to buy five more minutes from her parents to finish building a castle, read a story, make jewellery, and finish the game she started.

COMPREHENSION

A. Read the poem again and fill in the blanks.

1. Let me stay five .... more!
2. Can't I just finish the .... I'm reading here in my book?
3. It almost is finished, ...!
4. It's a pity never to find out whether you've .... or won.
5. Can't I stay .... minute more?

B. Answer the questions.

1. Name three things the child wants to do before bedtime.
2. Where is the child building the castle?
3. What does the child want to do after she has finished reading the book?
4. What makes the child sad about an unfinished game?

Life Skills and Values — Reflection and routine

1. What does the child actually mean when she says 'five minutes'? Does she only want to stay awake for five more minutes? Give reasons for your answer.
2. Here are some bedtime habits. Tick (✓) the ones you do.
   - ☐ brush my teeth
   - ☐ pack my school bag
   - ☐ keep my uniform and shoes ready
   - ☐ read/listen to a story
   - ☐ change my clothes
   - ☐ say a prayer

   What are the things that you feel are important to include in your routine? Tell your class.

Action words

- *Finish, read* and *build* are action words that are used in the poem. The words that define actions are called **action words**.
- Here are some more examples.
  laugh *play* *run* *paint* *sing*

A. Choose the action word in each set and circle it.

1. beautiful	rose	smell
2. boys	cry	flowers
3. cook	grandma	stove
4. dance	men	people
5. dog	kitten	bark
6. paint	picture	words
7. poem	poet	read
8. girls	shout	voice

B. Use the action words from the box to complete the sentences.

read *play* *eat* *wake up* *go* *talk* *brush* *listen* *laugh* *sleep*

1. We .... early in the morning.
2. We .... to school every day.
3. We .... with our friends in the playground.
4. We .... and .... with our parents.
5. We .... our dinner at night.
6. We .... to music.
7. We .... storybooks.
8. We .... our teeth.
9. We .... on time.

ACTIVITY

Make your bedtime clock using a paper plate.

Steps:

Cut out the hands and clock face. Colour the hands of the clock as per the colour key. Use a paper fastener to attach the hands to the face. Make sure the hands turn freely. Then glue the clock face onto a paper plate. Don't forget to show your bedtime in the clock.

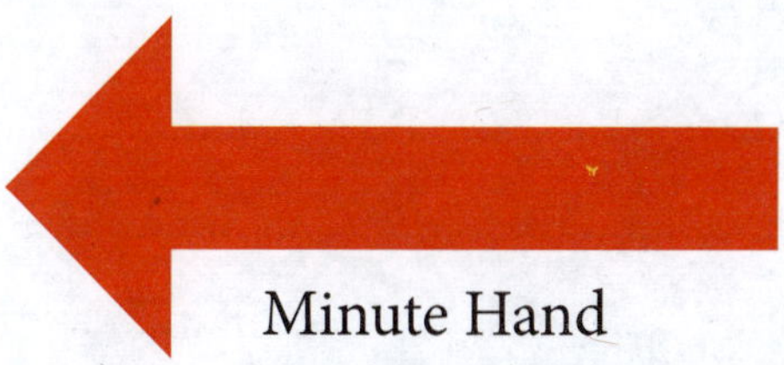

Minute Hand
Colour Red

Hour Hand
Colour Blue

9 Piklu and the Mynah

Empathy

OBJECTIVES

In this chapter, we will:

- *read the story of a boy who loves birds.*
- *learn synonyms and feeling words for non-human things.*
- *learn the simple present and the present continuous tenses.*
- *draw a picture to express thoughts.*
- *write our daily routine.*

WARM-UP

A. Look at the two sets of pictures carefully. Which set do you like better? Why? Share your thoughts by completing the given sentence.

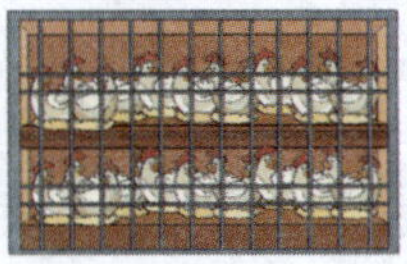  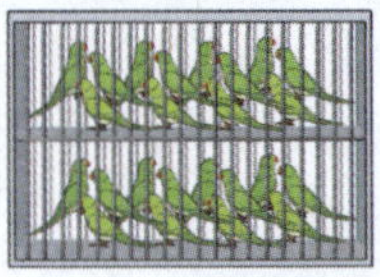 

Set A

Set B

I like Set .... *because* ....

....

....

B. Each one of us see things differently. Imagine if you were a bird, how would things appear to you from the sky? Match the pictures with their names.

1. buildings a. 

2. cars b. 

3. trees c. 

4. swings d. 

READING

Piklu loves animals and birds. Every morning he wakes up early to meet the birds in his garden. But one day he sees a bird in a cage. Read the story to find out what Piklu does.

Summer holidays are here! Piklu doesn't have to go to school. Still he wakes up early in the morning.

Rubbing his eyes he comes out in the garden. He is restless to hear the chirping of birds and to see them. His eyes begin to search the garden for them. At a careful glance he is able to spot a magpie, a sparrow, a bulbul, a parrot and many other birds.

One by one they greet him. Piklu begins to count them, 'One… two… three…' He moves further. Suddenly two yellow-beaked mynahs fly over his head.

Piklu becomes happy. He claps his hands with joy. The flowers swing their heads as if nodding in happiness. He can hear the bees humming cheerfully. Piklu plays with the birds all day long. He bathes them and feeds them too.

Next morning, Piklu sees a small mynah fluttering in a bird cage hanging from a tree. Its legs are tied to a chain.

restless: unable to relax
chirping: (of a bird) making short and sharp sounds
glance: look
spot: find
magpie: a long-tailed crow
bulbul: a songbird with a melodious voice
mynahs: small birds with a loud call
fluttering: (of a bird) flapping the wings quickly

He is shocked to see this. Piklu runs to his mother and asks, 'Who has caged the poor mynah, Ma?' He learns that his elder brother Toton caught it in the nearby forest.

Fact File

- Mynah's calls include chirps, clicks, croaks, and whistles.
- Mynahs can be trained to speak and even sing.

Piklu notices that the bird is sad and does not eat anything. Once in a while it gives out a sad cry. Piklu too feels sad for the bird. Hearing the mynah cry, no other bird comes to the garden. He wonders what to do. Then an idea strikes his mind! He brings a chair, climbs on it to reach the cage and unlocks it.

Piklu opens the chain tied to its leg and caresses the bird softly. Then he calls his mother who comes with an ointment. Mother applies some ointment to the bird's wounded leg.

The mynah feels better and chirps at Piklu. He lovingly teases the bird and teaches her to say his name. Soon the mynah learns to say, 'Pik-lu… Pik-lu'. Next, the mynah climbs up to a tree, and jumps from one branch to another. Finally she flies higher and higher into the vast expanse of the blue sky.

The red sun shines on the eastern sky. The flowers of the garden are blessed with the morning light. Dragonflies dance around. Bees and butterflies flutter over the colourful flowers. All of them are very happy.

But Piklu is worried. Will the mynah find her mother? Does she know the way to her home?

strikes: (here) a thought that comes to mind suddenly
unlocks: opens
caresses: touches gently
applies: puts
teases: (here) touches playfully
vast expanse: something that is spread out
dragonflies: fast-flying insects with two pairs of large transparent wings

Fact File

- *Tagar* is a flowering shrub found commonly throughout Southeast Asia.
- It is called the pinwheel flower in English because of its pinwheeled-shaped petals.
- It is known as *Chandni* in Hindi and *Nandiar Vattai* in Tamil.
- Parts of the plant are used to make medicines.

Next morning, Piklu hears someone calling him by his name. He rushes out. The mynah is sitting with its mother on the branch of a *tagar* shrub.

Piklu shouts with joy! Toton also comes out hearing his voice. He looks at the happy mynah. He feels sorry for putting it in a cage. He promises never to cage a bird in future.

SUMMARY

Piklu loves nature. Every morning, he plays with birds and bees in his garden. One day, he finds out that his brother has trapped a mynah in a cage. Along with his mother, he unchains the bird and puts ointment on its wounded leg. The mynah and Piklu soon become friends. Piklu even teaches the bird to say his name. The mynah flies now and then, but always comes back to meet Piklu.

COMPREHENSION

A. Choose the correct option.

1. Every morning Piklu wakes up and searches for .... in the garden.
   a. birds
   b. animals
   c. friends
2. .... fly over Piklu's head.
   a. Mynahs
   b. Two yellow-beaked parrots
   c. Sparrows

3. When Piklu sees the bird in the cage,
    a. he is sad.
    b. he is shocked.
    c. he gives it water.
4. Hearing the mynah cry,
    a. all birds gather around the crying bird.
    b. the mother bird comes to meet her baby.
    c. no other birds come to the garden.
5. Piklu shouts with joy because
    a. the mother gets an ointment.
    b. the mynah comes to meet him.
    c. Toton promises never to cage a bird in future.

B. Answer the questions.

1. What does Piklu search for every morning?
2. Name three birds that Piklu finds in the garden.
3. Who put the bird in the cage?
4. Where did the person get the bird from?
5. How did the bird show her unhappiness?
6. How did Piklu help the bird?
7. Who came back the next day? What was Piklu's reaction?
8. How does Toton feel when he looks at the happy mynah?

Life Skills and Values — **Empathy with animals**

1. Why do people keep pets? What do we have to keep in mind when we choose to keep pets? What do you think the pets feel? Discuss in small groups.
2. Do people who do not keep pets love animals? Give reasons to support your answer.

VOCABULARY

Synonyms

- Read these word pairs.

  big – large *small – tiny*

- Two words in each word pair mean the same. Such words are called **synonyms**.

A. Read the following words. Two of the words mean the same in each row. Circle them.

1. afraid	bold	scared	timid
2. cat	gift	present	skirt
3. clean	dirty	fresh	tidy
4. easy	hard	rich	simple
5. fast	quick	slow	stroll
6. murmur	shout	speak	whisper

Giving feelings to non-human things

- Sometimes we give feelings to things, plants and animals.
- It is also sometimes an extension of how we feel. For example:

  The wind howled loudly.

B. Read the following sentences. Underline the non-human thing and the action it does in each sentence.

1. The alarm clock shouted at me.
2. Rita heard the cake calling her.
3. A house is a friend that protects me.
4. The moon played hide-and-seek with the clouds.

GRAMMAR

Simple Present Tense

- The **simple present tense** is used to state facts. For example:

  Piklu *wakes* up early in the morning.

  He *claps* his hands with joy.

Mynah *moves* to the garden to climb up a tree.

The words *wakes*, *claps*, and *moves* are action words.

They tell us about an action which happens regularly.

The words are said to be in the simple present tense.

- The following chart describes how to use the simple present tense.
  - Add *-s* to most verbs
  - Add *-es* to verbs that end in *-ch*, *-o*, *-s*, *-sh*, *-x*, and *-z*. For example:

    watches, *does*, *kisses*, *washes*, *fixes*, *buzzes*

Positive sentence	
I	*go* (*verb*)
You	
They	
We	
He	*goes* (*verb + es*)
She	
It	

Negative sentence		
I	*do not* (*do verb + not*)	*go* (*verb*)
You		
They		
We		
He	*does not* (*do + -es + not*)	*go* (*verb*)
She		
It		

For example:

Piklu wakes up early. He goes to the garden.

His mother reads the newspaper. Then she goes to her office.

I/ They/ You go to school every day.

A. Read the following sentences. Fill in the blanks with the simple present form of the action words given in brackets.

1. We .... (*eat*) dinner together every day.
2. Mr Mann .... (*fly*) an aeroplane.
3. They .... (*play*) tennis every day.
4. The sun .... (*rise*) in the east.
5. Tina .... (*write*) with her left hand.

Present Continuous Tense

- We use the **present continuous** to refer to actions or events that are happening at the moment of speaking. For example:

  You *are reading* the textbook.

  The teacher *is speaking*.

  Everyone *is studying*.

- The present continuous is formed by adding *am/is/are* and *-ing* to action words.
- The following chart describes how to use the present continuous tense.

<table>
<tr><th colspan="3">Positive sentence</th><th colspan="4">Negative sentence</th></tr>
<tr><td>I</td><td>am</td><td rowspan="6">playing (verb+ing)</td><td>I</td><td>am</td><td rowspan="6">not</td><td rowspan="6">playing (verb+ing)</td></tr>
<tr><td>You</td><td>are</td><td>You</td><td>are</td></tr>
<tr><td>He/She</td><td>is</td><td>He/She</td><td>is</td></tr>
<tr><td>It</td><td>is</td><td>It</td><td>is</td></tr>
<tr><td>They</td><td>are</td><td>They</td><td>are</td></tr>
<tr><td>We</td><td>are</td><td>We</td><td>are</td></tr>
</table>

B. Read the following sentences. Fill in the blanks with the correct option.

1. Sona .... a storybook.
   a. am reading
   b. are reading
   c. is reading
2. Tara and Shreya .... for a holiday.
   a. am going
   b. are going
   c. is going
3. I .... with my toys.
   a. am playing
   b. are playing
   c. is playing

4. They .... lunch together.
   a. am cooking
   b. are cooking
   c. is cooking
5. We .... a movie.
   a. am watching
   b. are watching
   c. is watching

LISTENING AND SPEAKING

Listening

A. Listen to the description. Guess the name of the animal/bird/insect. Number them in the order in which you hear them.

- butterfly ☐
- duck ☐
- frog ☐
- mouse ☐
- spider ☐
- dog ☐

Speaking

21st CENTURY SKILLS
Communication

B. What kind of a place do you want to live in? Do you want to live in a forest, close to animals and birds? Or do you want to live surrounded by big houses, cars and buildings? Draw pictures and share your thoughts.

WRITING

Write your daily routine using the simple present form of action words given in the box.

brush *eat* *go* *play* *read* *study* *take* ~~*wake*~~ *watch*

I wake *up at 7 o'clock.*

Then I ....

After that I ....

....

When I come back from school, I ....

....

In the evening, ...

....

At night, I ....

....

Finally, ...

....

....

PROJECT 2

My Birdy Booklet

Go out with your parents. Watch the birds around your area. Make sure you do not disturb them. Take notes of what you see. Come back home and prepare a mini booklet with the details of at least three birds.

Date: ....

Time: ....

Name of the bird: ....

(Draw the bird in this box.)

(If you do not know the name of the bird, take help from adults or the Internet.)

This bird is also called .... in ....
(Write the name of the bird in any other language; also write the name of the language.)

The bird was ....
(Write the colour of the bird.)

The bird was ....
(Write if the bird was small or big.)

The bird was ....
(Write what the bird was doing.)

I saw the bird ....
(Write where you saw the bird.)

It was ....
(Write what sounds the bird was making.)

Folktale

10 The Water Seed

Community and Courage

OBJECTIVES

In this chapter, we will:

- *read the story of a young man who helps his village find water.*
- *learn to make compound words.*
- *learn the past simple and the past continuous tenses.*
- *learn to describe picture postcards.*
- *write an acrostic poem.*

WARM-UP

Mindfulness Activity
Sustainable living

A. **Go out into the open. Divide the class into teams of five. Each team makes a big circle. All teams are given one spoonful of water each. Next, without spilling even a drop of water, one member from each team carries the spoon to another member of the team. The first team to move the spoon of water among all its members wins.**

What did you learn from this activity? Discuss in class.

B. **Think of five things that you are thankful for. Tell your friends why you chose the things you did.**

C. **Have you ever wondered where water comes from? Look at the pictures given below. Unscramble the words to discover the sources of water.**

1. VRIRE ....

2. NSWO ....

3. EAKL ....

4. NIAR ....

12 RESPONSIBLE CONSUMPTION AND PRODUCTION

READING

When the rains did not come, the young men of the village went in search of water. One of them came back with a water seed! Read on and find out what happened next.

Long ago, in a village it did not rain for three years.

The earth was parched and all the plants dried up. The dry dust blew into people's eyes. They were very worried. They knew they could not live without water.

The village chief called for a meeting. Old and young, everybody came.

The chief asked four young men to come up.

He said, 'I want the four of you to go in four different directions to find water.'

parched: very dry due to hot weather and no rains
worried: unhappy or troubled about problems that might happen in the future

Earth Speak

- We can find water under the ground.
- This water comes mostly from rain, melted snow, and other water that seeps through soil, sand, or the cracks in the ground.
- Due to gravity, the water just keeps moving downward, underneath the Earth's surface, until it can't go any farther.
- Sometimes, groundwater can seep back up to the surface in form of springs and wetlands.

Three of them returned after some days, as they could not walk any further. The fourth one, who had gone north, reached a white mountain.

As he climbed up the slippery slope, he saw a cave. There was an old lady in the cave. 'Where can I find water?' the man asked her.

The old lady said, 'Go higher up on the mountain.'

The man climbed right to the top. He broke off a piece from the white mountain. He wrapped it carefully in a sack.

He ran back to the village as fast as he could.

When he got there, everyone ran to him to see what he got. He was very tired but happy. He said, 'I've brought back the water seed.'

When he opened his sack, the ice had melted into water! It dripped on to the ground and was absorbed by the soil.

With a cry, the villagers started digging to get back the water seed. They dug and they dug deeper. At last, they struck water!

slippery: something smooth, wet or oily and is therefore difficult to walk on or to hold
wrapped: covered in paper or soft material
dripped: water fell in small drops
absorbed: took in or soaked up (here, the soil took in the water)
struck: (here) found

Everyone shouted with joy, 'The water seed has given us water! The water seed has given us water!' And now the village had water.

They looked after it well. Now the village has water even if it does not rain.

SUMMARY

In a village, it did not rain for three long years. The chief sent out four young men in search of water. Three of them returned empty-handed but the fourth returned with a piece of the white mountain. He told the villagers that he has brought the water seed. When he opened the sack, the ice had melted into water. The villagers dug deep in search of the water seed and found water.

COMPREHENSION

A. Choose the correct option.

1. It did not rain for
   a. one year.
   b. two years.
   c. three years.

2. .... came for the meeting called by the village chief.
   a. Everybody
   b. Only old people
   c. Only young people
3. The young man met .... in the cave.
   a. a bear
   b. snow
   c. an old lady
4. The young man brought back .... from the mountain.
   a. a plant seed
   b. the old lady
   c. a water seed
5. When the villagers dug the ground, they found
   a. water.
   b. snow.
   c. a water seed.

B. Answer the questions.

1. What had happened to the earth and plants in the village?
2. Why were the people worried?
3. What did the village chief ask the four men to do?
4. Where did the fourth man go?
5. What did the old lady tell him?
6. What did the man get from the mountain?
7. What happened when he opened his sack? What was the reaction of the villagers then?
8. What did the villagers begin to do soon after?

Life Skills and Values — Courage and community

1. There are many places in the world that have been affected by heavy rains, storms, floods, landslides, earthquakes, etc. Find out about two such places.
2. How does help reach the affected areas? Who are the people who help in such situations? What qualities are displayed by such people? Do you see any of these qualities in you? Share your thoughts.

VOCABULARY

Compound words

- **Compound words** are single words that are formed by joining two different words. For example:

  rain + water → rainwater *pea + nut → peanut*

A. Use words from the box to make compound words. The pictures will help you.

bow	*brush*	*bug*	*fish*	*man*

1. jelly + ... → ....

2. lady + ... → ....

3. rain + ... → ....

4. snow + ... → ....

5. tooth + ... → ....

B. Fill in the blanks with the compound words that you have made.

1. I use my .... to clean my teeth.
2. A bright red .... sat on the leaf.
3. It is fun to make a .... on a snowy day.
4. You can't have a .... without a little rain.
5. .... live in the sea and look a little like umbrellas.

C. Make four compound words of your own.

1. ....

2. ....

3. ....

4. ....

GRAMMAR

Simple Past Tense

- We use the **simple past tense** to talk about things or actions which happened sometime in the past.
- The past could mean *an hour ago, yesterday, last night, two months ago, three years ago*, and so on.
- In many cases, the simple past is formed by adding *-ed* to the verb. For example:

  clean – cleaned *play – played* *walk – walked*

  I cleaned my room last Sunday.

  I walked to the park and played with my friends.

- But some verbs do not follow the *-ed* rule. For example:

Verb	Past tense
bring	*brought*
buy	*bought*
catch	*caught*
come	*came*
do	*did*
give	*gave*
go	*went*
have	*had*

Verb	Past tense
is	*was*
meet	*met*
see	*sawa*
sell	*sold*
sit	*sat*
teach	*taught*
win	*won*
write	*wrote*

- Some verbs remain the same in their simple past form. For example:

Verb	Past tense
cost	*cost*
cut	*cut*
hit	*hit*
hurt	*hurt*

Verb	Past tense
put	*put*
read	*read*
shut	*shut*
spread	*spread*

A. Read the following sentences from the story. Underline the verbs in the simple past tense.

1. All the plants dried up.
2. The village chief called for a meeting.
3. The man climbed right to the top.
4. He broke off a piece from the white mountain.
5. He wrapped it carefully in a sack.
6. He was very tired but happy.
7. It dripped on to the ground and was absorbed by the soil.
8. Everyone shouted with joy.

B. Fill in the blanks with the past simple form of the verbs in brackets.

1. It .... (*rain*) yesterday.
2. My mother .... (*lock*) the door.
3. Soha .... (*clean*) the blackboard.
4. I .... (*play*) with my friends this morning.
5. Aman .... (*give*) him a ball for his birthday.
6. She .... (*go*) to her uncle's house in holidays.
7. Everybody .... (*sit*) quietly to watch the play.
8. My friends.......................... (*come*) to my house last Saturday.

Past Continuous Tense

- We use the **past continuous tense** to talk about an action that was happening continually in the past.
- The past continuous is formed with *was* or *were* and the *–ing* form of the verb. For example:

  I was sleeping when it started to rain.

  Last night at 8 o'clock we were watching a movie.

C. Fill in the blanks with the past continuous form of the verbs in brackets.

1. She .... *(run)* to school.
2. It .... *(rain)* all morning.
3. They .... *(sit)* under a tree.
4. We .... *(stand)* in the snow.
5. Anna .... *(watch)* television.
6. Radha .... *(talk)* on the phone.
7. He .... *(write)* an email to his father.
8. The birds .... *(fly)* around the garden.

LISTENING AND SPEAKING

Listening

A. Listen to a short paragraph on the importance of water. Then fill in the blanks.

1. We need water for .... and .... (*Mention any two things.*)
2. .... per cent of the earth is covered with water.
3. Only .... per cent water is fresh and usable. The rest of the water is .... or is in the form of ....
4. We .... (*should/should not*) save water.

Speaking

21st CENTURY SKILLS Collaboration

B. Divide your class into six groups. Each group gets a picture postcard. Discuss the picture in your groups. Then briefly describe the picture to the class. Make sure the group presentation is in the order of the pictures given below.

1.

2.

3.

4.

5.

6.
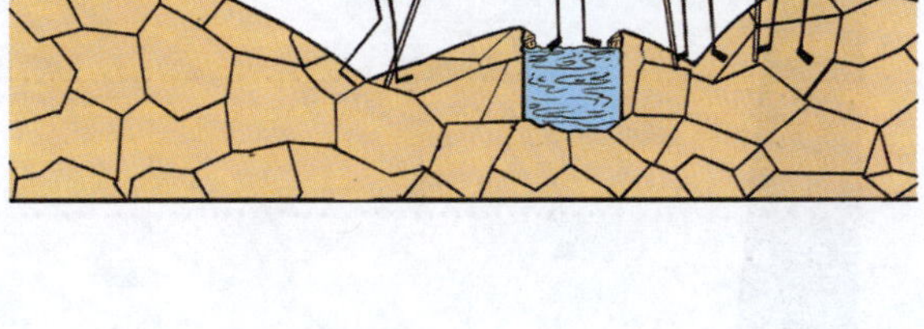

WRITING

Acrostic poem

- Poems are of different kinds.
- In an acrostic poem, the lines are formed by the first letters of the chosen word. For example:

Water on the rug,

Around the house and above!

Till the roof and in my cup,

Everywhere on the earth!

Run! Run! Run! It's a flood! It's a flood!

Write an acrostic poem with any one of the following words.

21st Century Skills — Creative Thinking

- TREE
- ANIMALS
- EARTH

11 The Two Kings

Character and Virtue

OBJECTIVES

In this chapter, we will:

- *read the story of a king who wants to know his faults.*
- *learn opposites and homophones.*
- *learn to use the joining words and and but.*
- *learn to use punctuation marks.*
- *enact a play.*
- *write a thank-you note.*

WARM-UP

Mindfulness Activity

Doing it right!

A. Close your eyes and take a deep breath. Think of at least three mindful things you did last week. Open your eyes. Read these actions. Tick (✓) which are mindful and which are not.

- ☐ Crossing the road after checking in both directions
- ☐ Leaving your socks on the floor when you come in from outside
- ☐ Helping a disabled person
- ☐ Interrupting someone while they are talking
- ☐ Criticising others but not thinking of your own bad habits
- ☐ Practising a new skill

B. Read the clues and fill in the crossword.

Across:

1. This is what a king's daughter is called
4. The chair on which a king sits
5. This is what a king's wife is called

Down:

1. A place where a king lives
2. A big animal that displays a king's power
3. A thing that a king wears on his head

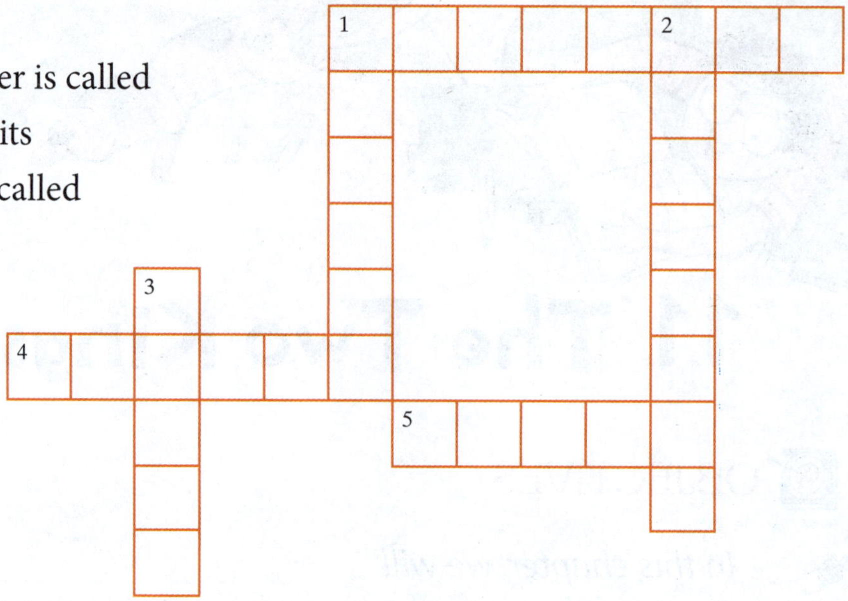

READING

Mallika, the king of Kosala is worried if he is as good as people say he is. One day, the king meets Brahmadatta, the king of Varanasi. Read the play to find out what happens next.

Narrator: Long, long ago a powerful and just king named Mallika once ruled over the Kingdom of Kosala. He had worked hard all his life and achieved great many things. But lately, he started doubting himself and kept thinking...

King Mallika: Am I really as good as people say I am?

Narrator: One day, he decided to call upon his trusted Minister and questioned him.

King Mallika: Tell me the truth. Is there no flaw in my character? Am I really that great?

Minister: Your Majesty, you are gentle, generous, kind and just. You have all the qualities a king should possess.

achieved: succeeded in something after a lot of effort
doubting: not trusting
flaw: a fault or weakness in someone's character
generous: a person who is friendly, helpful, and willing to see good qualities in others
just: morally correct

Narrator: King Mallika was still not satisfied with the answer. He decided to go into the town and ask the common people. There, in the marketplace, he met two men.

King Mallika: What would you say is my greatest fault?

Man 1: You have none, Your Majesty! You rule us wisely and well.

Man 2: Yes, indeed you do!

Narrator: The king just nodded and thought to himself.

King Mallika: Ministers and people are afraid to speak out. I'll go to the countryside where they do not recognise me.

Narrator: So, he sat on his royal elephant and set out. His mahout drove wherever he wished to go, but nowhere could he find a man who could point out his faults to him. They all said the same thing and chorused together.

People: There's no one as virtuous as our great King Mallika!

Narrator: The King went from one place to another and then one day he came to a narrow bridge. His royal elephant was about to cross the bridge when suddenly the mahout saw another royal elephant coming from the other side.

fault: a mistake for which someone is to be blamed
wisely: in a way that shows experience, knowledge, and good judgement
nodded: to move one's head up and down as a way of saying 'yes'
mahout: a person who rides and controls a domesticated elephant

Mahout 2: (*shouted*) Hold your horses. Let no one come in the way of my Royal Master, Brahmadatta, King of Varanasi.

Mahout 1: Well! My master is the King of Kosala. I cannot move aside for anyone.

Narrator: It was a practice in those days that the man of lower status should give the right of way to his superior.

Mahout 2: Both of us are carrying royal personages. Now who should move aside for whom?

Mahout 1: Let age or power decide that. How old is your master? How large is his kingdom?

Narrator: But it so happened that both the kings were of the same age and both their kingdoms were of the same size.

Mahout 2: Now what shall we do?

Mahout 1: Let the better man have the right of way.

Mahout 2: Who is the better man? What are your master's virtues?

Mahout 1: My master pays evil for evil and good for good.

Mahout 2: If those are your master's virtues, I shudder to think what his faults are.

Narrator: Hearing this, King Mallika thought to himself…

King Mallika: At last, I have met someone who is not afraid to speak his mind.

Mahout 1: Enough of your rudeness! Let's hear what your own master's virtues are.

personages: important or famous titles
shudder: to shake

King Mallika: That is something I would like to hear too.

Mahout 2: My master repays good for evil. He does good even to those who do him harm.

Narrator: As soon as King Mallika heard this, he got down from his royal elephant and bowed down to King Brahmadatta.

King Mallika: I salute you O King! Now I know what my faults are! Now I know how to refine myself.

Narrator: He turned towards his mahout.

King Mallika: Come let's draw our royal elephant and let King Brahmadatta pass.

Narrator: King Mallika looked on thoughtfully as King Brahmadatta's royal elephant passed by.

Fact File

- Elephants are the world's largest animals on land.
- Their trunk is amazing. It can pick up a peanut, shell it, blow the shell out and eat the nut.
- Elephants love to eat. They eat so much that they can spend three-quarters of their day eating.
- Elephants have a powerful memory. They never forget anything.

SUMMARY

The king of Kosala, Mallika wished to know whether he was a good king or not. He decided to personally meet the subjects of his kingdom and ask what they thought of him. Everyone praised him, but this did not satisfy the king. On another day, while crossing a bridge, he met Brahmadatta, the king of Varanasi. An argument followed between the two mahouts about who would cross the bridge first. It was decided that the person with better qualities shall cross the bridge first. During the conversation, King Mallika discovered that a good king is the one who remains his kind self even if others do not. He never forgets the goodness of his heart. The king finally gives way to King Brahmadatta for making him realise his faults.

COMPREHENSION

A. Answer the questions.

1. What did King Mallika doubt about himself?
2. What qualities did the Minister say the king had?

3. Why did the king go to the countryside?
4. What did King Mallika's mahout see when he was about to cross the bridge?
5. What was the other king's name? What kingdom did he rule?
6. What was the practice in those days?
7. What were the similarities between the two kings?
8. What was one virtuous quality that King Brahmadatta possessed but King Mallika did not?

B. Read the lines from the play and answer the questions.

1. *What would you say is my greatest fault?*
   a. Who is the speaker?
   b. What reply did he get?
2. *My master pays evil for evil and good for good.*
   a. Who is the speaker?
   b. Who is 'my master'?
3. *That is something I would like to hear too.*
   a. Who is the speaker?
   b. What does he want to hear?

Life Skills and Values — **Kindness and good character**

1. What would you do if a friend behaves badly with you? Would you be mean to them or show kindness? Why/Why not? Discuss in class.
2. Talk about the qualities a leader must have.

VOCABULARY

Opposites

- **Opposites** describe people or things that are completely different from each other. For example, *bad* is the opposite of *good*. Look at some more examples.

  more – less *buy – sell* *cry – laugh*

  happy – sad *small – big* *win – lose*

A. Choose the opposites of the underlined words from the box and fill in the blanks.

cheap *noisy* *old* *opens* *out* *soft*

1. The rock is <u>hard</u> but the feather is ....
2. The woman was .... but the man was <u>young</u>.
3. Every time I <u>close</u> the door, the dog .... it with his paw.
4. Everybody was <u>quiet</u> in the house but it was .... outside.
5. We got <u>in</u> through the front door and came .... from the back door.
6. She thought that the dress was <u>expensive</u> but it was actually ....

Homophones

- **Homophones** are words that have the same sound but different spellings. For example:

  I'll go to the countryside where they do not know me.

  Here, know means *to recognise someone.*

  Is there no flaw in my character?

  Here, no means *any.*

- Look at some more examples:

  I have only one pencil.

  I won the match easily.

  Here, one is *a number*, while won refers to *winning in the past.*

B. Circle the correct homophone and complete the sentence.

1. He .... (*ate/eight*) an apple.
2. The sky is clear and .... (*blew/blue*).
3. The whale lives in the .... (*sea/see*).
4. The .... (*son/sun*) is shining brightly.
5. There was a .... (*be/bee*) sitting on the flower.
6. There are .... (*too/two*) umbrellas in the cupboard.
7. We spent the .... (*hole/whole*) day cleaning the garden.
8. I am going to my grandparents' place for a .... (*weak/week*).

GRAMMAR

Joining words: *and* and *but*

- **Joining words** join two words or sentences together.
- *And* is a joining word. For example:

  My master pays evil for evil.

  My master pays good for good.

  To join the two sentences together, we can say:

  My master pays evil for evil and *good for good.*
- We use *but* to join two words or sentences that express opposite ideas. For example:

  The box is big.

  The box is not heavy.

  To join the two sentences together, we can say:

  The box is big but *not heavy.*

A. Use the joining word *and* to combine the sentences in each pair.

1. Alice fell down. Alice hurt her feet.

   ....

2. Dina wakes up early. Dina goes for a walk.

....

3. My father baked a cake. My father baked some cookies.

....

4. Arya will eat pasta for lunch. Arya will eat bread for lunch.

....

5. Riddhi helped Shona with homework. Riddhi helped Vidhi with homework.

....

B. Use the joining word *but* to combine the sentences in each pair.

1. Meenu is short. Rahul is tall.

....

2. The TV is on. No one is watching it.

....

3. Tina likes to sing. She cannot dance.

....

4. Radha fell down. She did not get hurt.

....

5. I went to Ayub's house. He was not at home.

....

Punctuation

- We use special marks while writing, called **punctuation marks**.
- When we speak, we pause after a complete **sentence**.
- When we write, we put a **full stop** (.) at the end of a sentence.
  For example:

  I have an English class today.

Question mark

- When we ask for information, we change the way we speak.
- This helps the listener understand that we are asking a **question**.
- When we write, we put a **question mark** (?) at the end of a sentence. For example:

  Can I sit here?

  Do we have a holiday tomorrow?

Exclamation mark

- When we express surprise, shock, anger or warning, we change the way we speak.
- When we write, we put an **exclamation mark** (!) at the end of a sentence. For example:

  Watch out! There is a car coming.

  Hurray! Our team won the inter-school championship trophy!

C. Read the following sentences. Use a full stop (.)/a question mark (?)/ an exclamation mark (!) at the end of each sentence.

1. The sun shines in the morning
2. Where is my apple
3. What a beautiful day
4. Who lives in that house
5. I am so happy to have a new dress
6. Can you ride the red bike
7. A bee makes sweet honey
8. I am working on my science project

LISTENING AND SPEAKING

Listening

A. Listen to the story and fill in the blanks.

1. Once there lived a king with his .... sons.
2. He asked his sons to .... the entire room with something.
3. The first son hurriedly went into the treasure room and filled the room with .... and diamonds.
4. The third son kept a .... in the middle of the room.

Speaking

B. In groups, enact the roles of the narrator, the two mahouts and the two kings.

Remember:

- You don't have to memorise the dialogues; just read them out.
- Use proper expressions and gestures.
- Have control over the speed, style and tone of your voice to make clear dialogue delivery.
- Rehearse before you perform.

WRITING

Complete this thank-you note for someone whose qualities you admire.

Dear ....,

Thank you for ....

....

....

I wish to tell you that ....

....

....

I think you are ....

because ....

....

.... *(your name)*

12 The Kite

Exploration

OBJECTIVES

In this chapter, we will:
- *read and enjoy the poem.*
- *learn about words related to wind.*
- *spot differences between pictures.*

WARM-UP

Mindfulness Activity
Be in charge!

A. Stand like a surfer. Your teacher will tell you how to!
Then count till ten while taking calm breaths.
Then shake your legs and stand on the other side.
Do you feel all your unhappy and sad thoughts getting absorbed by the ground?

Remember to be aware of how your thoughts make you feel. Watch them and let them go.

B. Think of at least two things or people in your life that bring you happiness. Write a sentence on each.

....

....

C. Imagine you are a kite and you are flying over the following places. Unscramble the words and identify the places.

1. OMUTANISN .... 2. REIVR .... 3. ICYT ....

READING

A little child wishes to become a kite and travel to many places. Let's read the poem by Frank Dempster Sherman and find out where all he wishes to travel.

I often sit and wish that I,
Could be a kite up in the sky.
And ride upon the breeze and go,
Whatever way I chanced to blow.
Then I could look beyond the town,
And see the river winding down.
And follow all the ships that sail,
Like me, before the merry gale.
Until at last with them I came,
To some place with a foreign name.

breeze: a gentle wind
chanced: to do something without planning
merry: happy
gale: a very strong wind
foreign: unfamiliar, strange

SUMMARY

The poet talks about travelling the world just as the kite. He wants to ride along with the winds. Excited to see the world from above, he wants to look down upon the sailing ships and the flowing river. In the end, he wishes to reach a place that he has never seen before.

COMPREHENSION

A. Mark the sentences as true (T) or false (F).

1. The poet wants to ride upon the breeze. ☐
2. The poet wants to look beyond the sailing ships. ☐
3. The poet is afraid to travel to unknown places. ☐
4. In the end, the poet wants to get back home. ☐

B. Answer the questions.

1. What does the poet wish to be?
2. Name three things that the poet would see from the top.
3. Do you think the poet is bored of living in the same place? Why/Why not?

Life Skills and Values

Imagination and travel

1. If you could fly, where would you like to go and why? Tell your friends.
2. Do you like visiting new places and meeting new people? Why/Why not? Discuss in class.

VOCABULARY

Words related to wind

- Winds are of different kinds.
- The poet in the poem uses words such as *breeze* and *gale* to describe the movement of wind.
- While breeze is *gentle*, gale is *strong*.

A. Match the names of winds with their pictures.

1. breeze

a. 

2. tornado

b. 

3. storm

c. 

B. Can you find the words in Exercise A in the word grid given below?

T	O	R	N	A	D	O
S	T	O	R	M	W	C
H	N	P	U	F	F	Y
I	L	B	L	E	R	G
B	R	E	E	Z	E	A
W	E	R	T	Y	O	E
C	E	C	L	V	G	L

ACTIVITY

Spot eight differences in the two pictures.

13 Travelling to Assam

Country and Travel

OBJECTIVES

In this chapter, we will:

- *read a travelogue on a journey to Assam.*
- *learn travel words and arrange words in alphabetical order.*
- *learn to use am, is, are and -wh questions.*
- *learn to ask for and give directions.*
- *write a postcard.*

WARM-UP

Mindfulness Activity
Finding your soul

A. Sit comfortably and close your eyes. Think of a place in nature where you can visit anytime. While you are there, think of these factors:

- What is there?
- How's the weather?
- Do you have your favourite food there?
- What does the place look like?
- What do you enjoy doing there?
- Does it have a smell?
- How did you feel the last time you were there?

Come back into the present. How do you feel when you open your eyes?

B. What does the word *travel* remind you of? Write down the words that come to your mind.

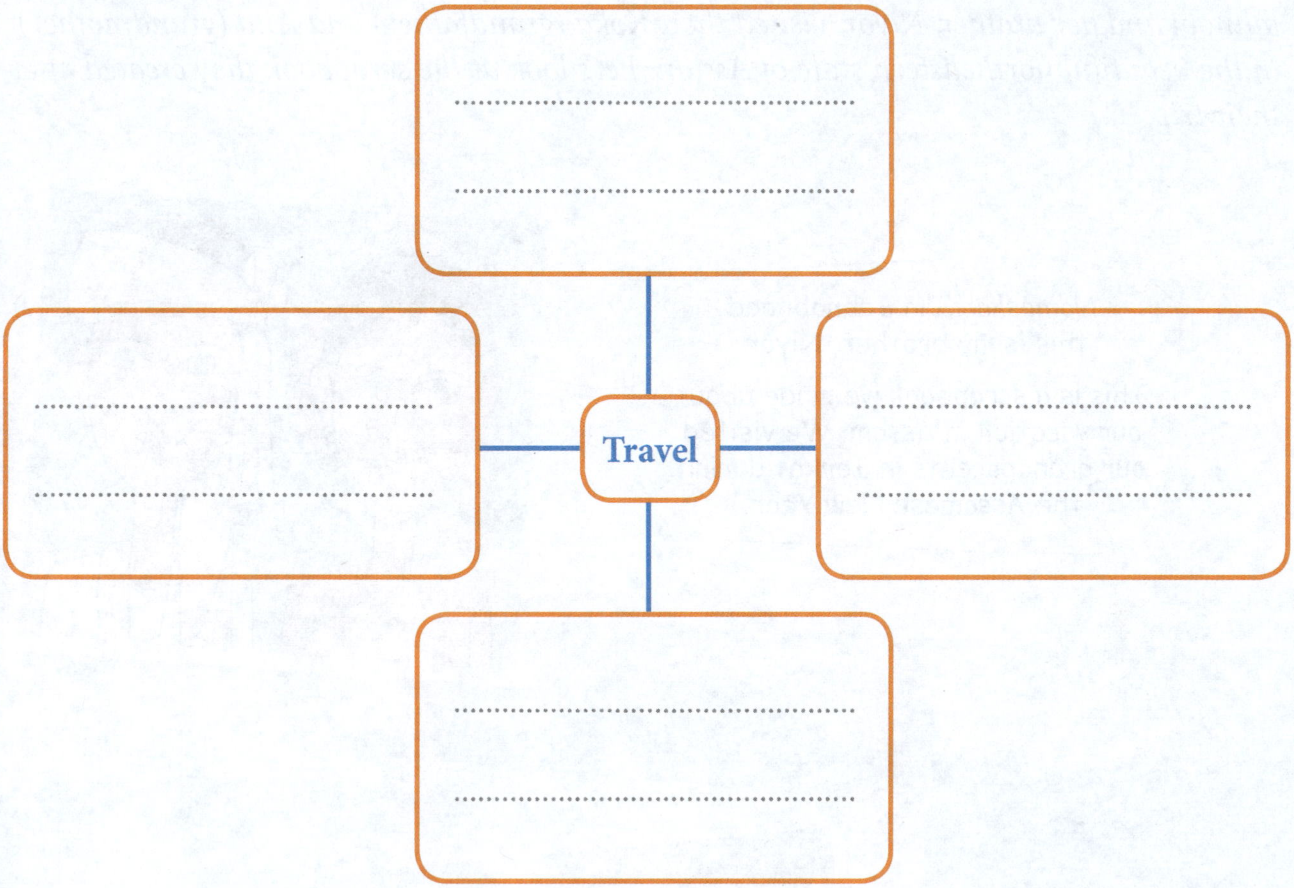

READING

Jahnobi and her brother, Niyor, visited their Koka (grandfather) and Aita (grandmother) in the beautiful northeastern state of Assam. Let's look at the scrapbook they created after their trip.

Nomoskar! I'm Jahnobi and this is my brother, Niyor.

This is a scrapbook we made about our vacation in Assam. We visited our grandparents in Jorhat during the Assamese New Year.

Earth Speak

- Assam is situated in the eastern Himalayas.
- Dispur is the capital of Assam.
- Guwahati is the largest city in the state.
- Guwahati is also known as the Gateway to the Northeast.
- The Brahmaputra flows through Assam.
- Assamese is spoken in Assam.

We stayed at our grandparents' tea estate. Assam is famous for its tea gardens. Our *Aita* told us that Assam tea is popular across the world.

This is a picture of the *Bohag Bihu* festival we celebrated with our family. It is the main festival of Assam. It is celebrated in the month of April. It marks the Assamese New Year. We sing *Bihu geets* or songs to the beats of the *dhol*. We dance with a *Jappi*, the traditional conical bamboo hat.

We dressed in traditional clothes gifted to us by our grandparents. I wore a *mekhela-chador*. A *mekhela* is a skirt and a *chador* is a long piece of cloth pleated and tucked into the *mekhela*. Niyor wore a *dhoti* and a *gamusa* or a traditional towel.

Our Favourite Assamese Food:

Healthy and tasty!

***Masor tenga** is* fish curry cooked in a broth made with tomato, *outenga* (elephant apple) and lemon. It is eaten with rice.

Aloo pitika is a simple dish eaten with rice and *dal*. It is made of mashed or crushed potatoes mixed with mustard oil, onion, coriander and salt.

Pitha is a snack made of rice. It can be cooked in different ways–sweet or salty, steamed or fried. It is usually eaten during breakfast or evening tea.

Postcards from Assam...

Our day trip to Kaziranga National park

We rode an elephant and saw a lot of wild animals like the great Indian one-horned rhinoceroses, royal Bengal tigers, and golden langurs.

Weekend trip to Sivasagar

One weekend, we travelled to the town of Sivasagar to see Rang Ghar. It has Asia's first amphitheatre. In the past, it served as the royal sports building where kings and nobles watched buffalo fights and other sports.

A visit to Guwahati

We also went to Guwahati to pray at the Kamakhya Temple. It was built around 1100 to 1200 years ago!

We also bought beautiful silks, bamboo, and cane products as gifts for our friends back home.

SUMMARY

This is a travel scrapbook of Jahnobi and Niyor about their trip to Assam. During their vacation, they visit their grandparents and stay at their tea estate. They wear traditional clothes, eat their favourite Assamese foods and celebrate *Bohag Bihu* together. They also take a day trip to Kaziranaga National park and spend a weekend in Sivasagar to see Rang Ghar, Asia's first amphitheatre. They also travel to Guwahati to pray at the Kamakhya Temple. On their way, they buy silks and bamboo, and cane products for their friends.

COMPREHENSION

A. Mark the sentences as true (T) or false (F).

1. Assam is situated in South India. ☐
2. Assam is famous for coffee plantations. ☐
3. *Bohag Bihu* celebrates the Assamese New Year. ☐
4. *Aloo Pitika* is eaten with rice and *dal*. ☐

B. Answer the questions.

1. What do women and men wear in Assam?
2. What did Jahnobi and Niyor do at the Kaziranga National Park?
3. Where is Rang Ghar located?
4. Name any two dishes of Assam.
5. Why do you think the author calls Assamese food healthy?

Life Skills and Values — Travel and knowledge

1. What are the things that you would need to take along on your trip to each of these places?
   a. the beach b. the desert c. the mountains
2. What factors will help you decide that? Explain to your class.

VOCABULARY

A. Read the sentences and choose the correct words from the box.

camera *hotel* *restaurant* *suitcase* *tent* *train*

1. We pack our things in it. ....
2. While camping, we stay in this. ....
3. While travelling, we usually eat at this place. ....
4. When we go on a holiday, we often stay here. ....
5. We capture memories by clicking pictures with this. ....
6. We sometimes use this means of transport for travelling. ....

B. Use the words from the above exercise to fill in the blanks.

Last summer, we went for a holiday to Shimla by .... We stayed in a .... there. There was a good .... where we had some Himachali food. We decided to go camping and we packed our clothes in a .... We spent the night in a .... on the foothills of the Himalayas. It was an amazing experience. In the morning, we took a lot of pictures with our .... It was a great holiday.

Alphabetical order of words starting with the same letter

- Read these words:

  train, ticket, tent, torch
- They all begin with *t*.
- To arrange these words in alphabetical order:
  - look at the second letter of each word
  - arrange the words according to the order of the second letter
  - So, the alphabetical order of these words is:

  tent, ticket, torch, train

C. Arrange the words in alphabetical order.

1. land leg lost light

....

2. boy bell baby bread

....

3. ant apple alligator aeroplane

....

4. cot cat crow clip

....

5. pit pup plum parrot

....

6. egg eel enemy elephant

....

GRAMMAR

Using *am, is, are*

- We use *am* with the pronoun *I*. For example:

  *I **am*** a girl. *I **am*** a boy.

- We use *is* with *he*, *she*, *it* or a naming word that is only one in number. For example:

  *She **is** naughty.* *It **is** my pencil.*

  *My mother **is** a doctor.* *The peacock **is** a beautiful bird.*

- We use *are* with *we*, *you*, or *they* and with naming words which mean more than one in number. For example:

  *We **are** students.* *You **are** smart.*

  *They **are** in the room.* *The children **are** singing.*

A. Fill in the blanks with *am, is* or *are*.

1. I .... seven years old.
2. We .... happy today.
3. It .... made of wood.
4. Rita .... my best friend.

5. She .... a Hindi teacher.
6. They .... making too much noise.
7. These beds .... comfortable.
8. My grandfather .... a farmer.

Questions with *wh-* words

- We use the ***wh***-words *what*, *where*, *when*, *who*, and *why* to ask questions.
- ***What*** is used to ask about a thing or an action. For example:
  What is on the table? *What are you doing?*
- ***Where*** is used to ask about a place or position. For example:
  Where is the table? *Where are you going?*
- ***When*** is used to ask about the time, day, month, year, and so on. For example:
  When do you go to your grandparents' place?
  When do we celebrate Diwali?
- ***Who*** is used to ask about people. For example:
  Who is in the room? *Who is shouting there?*
- ***Why*** is used to ask about the reason for something. For example:
  Why are you sad? *Why is the shop closed today?*

B. Fill in the blanks with the correct question word.

1. .... is in the box?
2. .... are you crying?
3. .... is your father going?
4. .... is your brother's name?
5. .... will make breakfast today?
6. .... are you going for a holiday?
7. .... do you have winter vacation?
8. .... will help you with homework?

C. Fill in the blanks with the suitable question word and *am, is* or *are*.

1. Question: .... Mumbai?
   Answer: It's in India.

2. Question: .... on the table?

Answer: That is my storybook.

3. Question: .... Mr R.N. Kovind?

Answer: He is the 14th president of India.

4. Question: .... your birthday?

Answer: It's tomorrow.

5. Question: .... you running?

Answer: I am late for school.

LISTENING AND SPEAKING

Listening

A. Listen to a conversation and mark the sentences as true (T) or false (F).

1. Mona is going to Nainital during the summer vacation. ☐
2. She is going there with her grandparents. ☐
3. Mona and her family will travel by train. ☐
4. They will live in a small cottage there. ☐
5. They plan to go boating there. ☐

Speaking

21st CENTURY SKILLS
Communication

B. Work in pairs. Taking turns, ask for and give directions to reach the school library from your classroom. Use these clues.

Asking for directions
• *Can you tell me the way to .... from here?* • *Do you know the way to ....?*
Giving directions
• *Go straight.* • *Turn right/turn left.* • *On the right, you will find ..../ on the left, you will find ....*

WRITING

Postcard writing

- Postcards are cards with a picture on one side.
- Always think of the person you are writing the postcard to, and choose a picture postcard he/she would love.
- The back of the postcard is usually split in two. The address and the message are written at the back. We do not write anything in the front.
- Write the receiver's full address on the right side of the postcard, and your message on the left.
- Place the stamp on the top right of the postcard.
- Write the date on the top left side of the postcard.
- Your message needs to fit within the left side of the postcard, and hence must be short. You may use colourful pens to write a message.
- Sign your name on the bottom left of the postcard. You may also add the name of the place you're writing from.
- Postcards are sent without an envelope.
- Many stationery and gift shops sell postcards. They are also sold everywhere in popular tourist areas.

Write a postcard to your friend who lives in a faraway city. Your message could be about anything. Study the sample and make a similar postcard in your notebook.

22 December 2021

Dear Deb,

Today I saw the white desert under the moonlight, and I wish you were here to see how breathtaking it looked! I'll be visiting you this New Year's Eve. See you soon!

Give my love to uncle and aunty!

Love,
Jenny
Rann of Kutch, Gujarat

34, Himkunj Lands
Mazatec Towers, Sector 54
Delhi 112233

PROJECT 3

My Last Holiday

Write a travel journal entry about your recent holiday.

The weather was...

....

....

I ate...

....

....

Five things I did on my holiday...

....

....

....

....

....

Fun Time!

A. These animals look lost. Draw the path and help them reach their homes.

B. Play the board game of Snakes and Ladders. After playing one round of game, answer the questions that follow.

1. How many numbers are there in this board game? ....
2. If a player lands at number 13, he/she will climb to number ....
3. If a player lands at number 76, he/she will drop to number ....
4. Circle the longest ladder in the picture. By how many numbers will it take you up? ....
5. By how many numbers will the longest snake bring you down? ....

C. **Look at these road signs on the road. Read their meanings in the box and write the number of the correct meaning next to the sign.**

1. School Ahead *2. One Way* *3. Trucks Prohibited*

4. Horn Prohibited *5. Zebra Crossing* *6. Speed Limit*